Perth's Trams *and* Early Buses

A.W. Brotchie

Stenlake Publishing Ltd

© Alan Brotchie, 2019.
First published in the United Kingdom, 2019,
by Stenlake Publishing Ltd.,
54-58 Mill Square,
Catrine, Ayrshire,
KA5 6RD

Telephone: 01290 551122
www.stenlake.co.uk

Printed by Blissetts, Roslin Road, Acton, W3 8DH

ISBN 9781840338249

The publishers regret that they cannot supply copies of any pictures featured in this book.

Cherrybank terminus *c*1904 with car 1, now in Corporation ownership. The driver is John Bruce, source of many anecdotes, his youthful conductor is Geordie Buchan. The car is one of the original fleet, the 'join' where it has been extended from four windows to six being apparent.

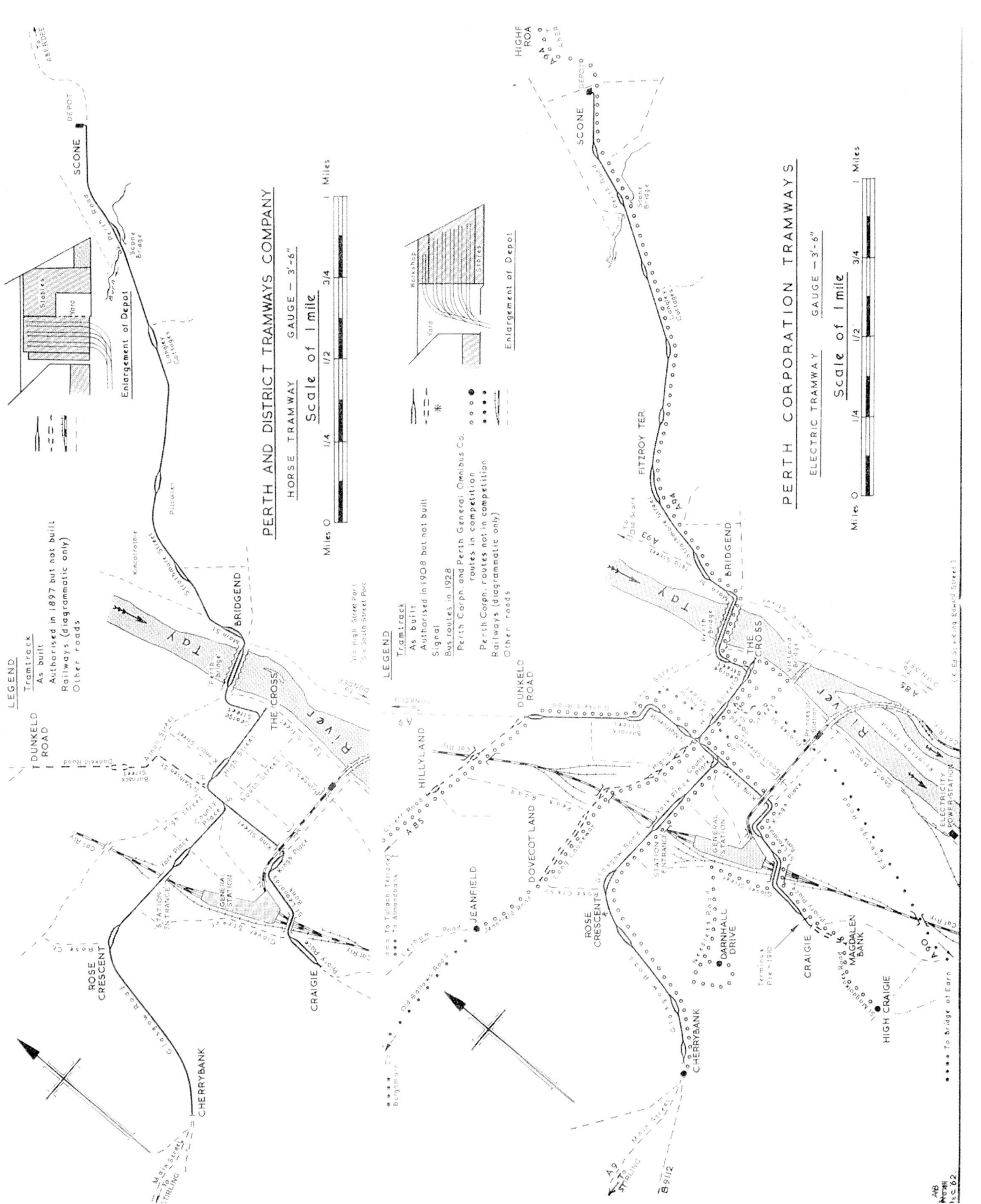

Preface

The story of local transport in the City of Perth has interested me since I lived in Scone some years ago and had a basic history included in my *Tramways of the Tay Valley*. I examined the official minutes and contemporary newspapers, but relevant papers held by Perth Town Council have since then been deposited in Perth and Kinross Archives and have now been fully studied, adding considerable detail. At the time I did my original research I was able to meet men who had served during the earliest years of public transport in Perth, such as John Bruce who commenced work as a horse tram driver on 1st January 1896 and spent his entire career with the local tram then bus undertaking. His memories of early years were crystal clear and operational details were recalled which were not available from the written record; it was a privilege to meet him.

I have attempted to ensure as little duplication with that earlier work as possible. There is no desire here to list every individual bus used by W Alexander in Perth, the major operator after 1934. Specialist publications such as those by Allan T Condie, the P S V Circle and the Omnibus Society fulfil that purpose and are available for anybody seeking such intimate detail.

For this work several individuals have given generously of their time and specialist knowledge; thanks must be recorded to Ian Bruce, Allan Condie, Alan Findlay, Richard Gadsby, Gerald Hartley, Geoff Lumb, Graham Martin-Bates, D N M Paton, Alan Simpson, John Sinclair, I A Souter and the patient and knowledgeable staff of Perth's A K Bell Library and Archives Departments.

For a subject of this nature illustrative material is not inexhaustive and some illustrations have been reproduced previously; I hope the reader will show understanding. I have attempted to ascertain correct attribution for photographs; if any are incorrectly acknowledged I apologise – and will correct in any reprint. Also, if anybody is aware of material relevant to the history of Perth's early transport, I would be very pleased to hear from them.

'Early' in the title has no precise definition; generally speaking it means the end of the 'red bus' era in the City *c*1963, but the arrival – and rapid departure – of an unexpected tram in the 21st century deserves at least a mention.

Introduction

The location chosen by prehistoric settlers to establish a permanent settlement by the side of the River Tay was not a matter of chance, but then such matters seldom were. It was most probably the highest point on the tidal river where, at periods of low water, the river was fordable, originating today's City of Perth. In the centre of Scotland, its significance grew slowly but steadily following the Roman incursions of two millennia past. The Romans bridged the Tay with a wooden structure just north of the confluence with the River Almond and remains of the timber structure were said still to be visible at the start of the 19th century. This significant locus was also the highest normal tidal reach and may have become a port serving a large hinterland. Although the name 'Bertha' was contrived in relatively recent times for the Roman settlement, it is considered more likely to have been named 'Tamia' by them. This name is shown on Ptolomey's *Geographia* atlas, from the second century, which is understandably vague in its depiction of Caledonia, the most distant element of the Roman Empire.

Scone Abbey was founded on the east side of the Tay almost opposite the site of the former Roman camp and close to the associated north-heading road. By the 9th century the abbey was the accepted setting for coronations of Scotland's kings using the famous Stone of Scone (believed now to be in Edinburgh Castle following return from Westminster Abbey in 1996); 38 kings of Scots were crowned here. Through succeeding centuries Perth grew, as a consequence of its strategic position, into one of Scotland's most important trade and market centres being elevated to the status of Royal Burgh by King David I during the 12th century, thence acting as effective capital of the Kingdom until 1437. Through the Middle Ages it prospered, expanding into a trading centre for the produce of the surrounding fertile countryside. Its situation and demeanor earned it the happy sobriquet of the 'Fair City' following publication in 1828 of Sir Walter Scott's novel *The Fair Maid of Perth*.

The Roman timber bridge did not survive long, and it was not until the 13th century that there is found a mention – in a Scone Charter of 1219 – of an arched stone bridge, crossing the river on the approximate extended line of the High Street. This was but the first in a succession of such structures, each one unable to resist the floodwaters of the river in spate. In all there are thought to have been five bridges here or hereabouts, the last one succumbing to floods in 1621 (supposedly the result of the iniquity of the town's inhabitants). After this travelers had to resort to ferries, of which up to thirty were employed, the dangerous crossing leading to much risk and loss of life amongst both ferrymen and passengers. Despite these difficulties it was not until the middle of the following century that efforts were made to fund a replacement, the campaign led by Thomas Hay, Earl of Kinnoull. Government funds, meeting half the cost, came mostly from estates of dispossessed Jacobite supporting lairds. Construction commenced in 1768 about 350 yards upstream from the earlier site, completed in just over three years. This handsome structure of pink sandstone was designed by John Smeaton – who had also been responsible for the rather similar 1763-67 bridge over the River Tweed at Coldstream which, like the bridge on the Tay, still stands, both carrying 21st century traffic. The arches over the Tay were completed in 1771, with a roup of the timber centering held on 30th of October that year. The bridge, at that time the longest in Scotland, was not opened until the following February and the tack of the toll charge (or pontage) was not in place until Whitsunday 1772. The plaque on the bridge giving a date of 1768 is at best misleading. In 1869 the bridge was widened, the stone parapets removed and new footpaths built on cantilevered cast iron brackets, with new cast iron parapets. The toll charge of ½d lasted until 1883.

Victoria Bridge, extending the line of South Street, opened in 1902 to alleviate traffic on the Old Bridge and it in its turn was replaced in 1960 by the present Queen's Bridge, the first long-span prestressed concrete bridge in Scotland.

By the reign of William IV Perth was well connected to the rest of Scotland by numerous stagecoach operations, detailed on the accompanying extract from an 1845 directory, but this was all to change following arrival of railways in 1847. Initially the first of these reached only to Barnhill on the east bank of the Tay, with the opening of the Dundee & Perth line on 24th May. The continuation of the journey into town was made by omnibus via Bridgend, this the earliest regular local operation so far uncovered. John Ross's *Wonder* coach was taken off its Dundee to Perth run, henceforth running from Perth to Dunkeld and Aberfeldy. The following year saw the mushrooming of local railways and the foundation laid for Perth's status as a major rail intersection and junction. The Scottish Central Railway opened through to Stirling in May, the Edinburgh & Northern to Ladybank and on to the Forth Ferry at Burntisland for Edinburgh in July followed in August by the first length of the Aberdeen line, opened by the Scottish Midland Junction Railway as far as Forfar. With

Left: As a major centre Perth had a remarkable number of stage coach connections. This list of departures dates from 1846.

the new General Station for use by all companies built on the western extremity of the town, the opportunity was grasped by hotel proprietors to provide small omnibuses to meet trains and convey their clients, and any others, into town, and to their respective establishments. Feeder omnibuses ran from rail termini to Perthshire towns, with as early as 1852, Robert Reid of the Athole [sic] Arms in Auchtergaven [Bankfoot] from 1st July running a regular coach in to Perth. The following summer the Commercial Inn owner ran daily from Bridge of Earn to Dunkeld, returning later the same day, a facility greatly appreciated by that new phenomenon, the day tripper.

Scone & Perth Omnibus Company Limited (1863-1893)

SCONE AND PERTH OMNIBUS COMPANY (LIMITED).

TIME BILL.

LEAVES SCONE FOR GENERAL STATION, PERTH.
On Monday, Tuesday, Thursday, and Saturday, at 8.30, A.M.; 2.15, P.M.; and 6.0, P.M.
On Wednesday and Friday, at 8.30, A.M.; 2.15, P.M.; and 7.0, P.M.

GENERAL STATION FOR BARNHILL.
On Monday, Tuesday, Thursday, and Saturday, at 9.15, A.M.; 2.45, P.M.; and 7.10, P.M.
On Wednesday and Friday, at 9.15, A.M.; and 2.45, P.M.

BARNHILL FOR GENERAL STATION.
On Monday, Tuesday, Thursday, and Saturday, at 9.45, A.M.; 3.40, P.M.; and 7.20, P.M.
On Wednesday and Friday, at 9.45, A.M.; and 3.40, P.M.

GENERAL STATION FOR SCONE.
Daily, at 12.30, P.M.; 4.5, P.M.; and 8.10, P.M.

BALBEGGIE,
FOR SCONE, BRIDGEND, AND PERTH.
Every Wednesday and Friday, at 8.0, A.M.
Returning from General Station, Perth, same days, at 4.5, P.M.

Note.—The 'Bus leaving Scone at 2.15, P.M. and Perth for Barnhill at 2.45, P.M. will stop and start from Mr. COCHRANE's, 127, High Street.

FARES.

FROM	IN.	OUT.	FROM	IN.	OUT.
Balbeggie to Scone,	6d	4d	Scone to Perth,	4d	3d
Balbeggie to Perth,	9d	6d	Scone to General Station,	6d	4d
Scone to Bridgend,	2d	2d	Perth to Barnhill,	2d	3d
Gen. Station to do.	3d	3d	General Station to Town,	2d	2d

Every attention will be given to the despatch and delivery of Parcels, which may be left at the Receiving Office, 127, High Street, Perth.

Above: The first published timetable of the Scone & Perth Omnibus Co dating from 1863.

Formation of a company to run an omnibus between Scone and the General Station was publicly debated during April 1863. A company was rapidly put in place with shares made available with a physical start planned for mid-May, but which probably started on 1st June. The driving force was Mr. J S Greenfield, general merchant, of Scone – whose dedication to the project was recognised two years later by presentation of a fine chiffonnier for his efforts. The initial capital was £500 in £1 shares, of which £130 was taken up by 68 (mostly local) investors, by June. The incumbent minister of Scone Free Church and his wife both took ten shares, with the largest individual subscriber James Mitchell, draper in Scone, who by 1873 had become Company Chairman. The bus ran to the Station entrance on Glasgow Road, with its route extended to Balbeggie as indicated on the advert above.

Thirty years of beneficial public service was mostly without incident. However, the most unfortunate episode recorded was on a dark night in October 1885 when a youthful passenger, George Hamilton, sitting innocently outside on the bus by the stables at the top end of Scone, was shot accidentally and died from his injuries. Fifteen year-old conductor John Galletly had been asked by local man William Haggart to hold his shotgun while he lifted a dog on to the vehicle – but what had not been said was that the gun was loaded in both barrels. Although Haggart swore that the safety catch was locked, the gun was somehow accidentally discharged by Galletly, with fatal consequences. Haggart was charged with culpable homicide but found not guilty by a jury.

Seemingly run more as a public service than for creating profit, the undertaking ran at a small loss for many years, until eventually in 1881-82 a profit of £11.12s.11 ½d was achieved. The following year patient shareholders benefitted from their first dividend, of 5%. This marked a turning point; subsequent years seeing regular returns of 7½%, allowing purchase of a new lighter bus in 1884-85; it was then that the first suggestion was aired that a tram might be an improvement on the bus. A return of 12½% achieved in 1888-89 led to more talk of a tram line, the outcome being the formation in March 1892 of a company to achieve this. All was arranged in a civilised manner, with an agreement arrived at for the transfer of the bus businesses property, fixtures and fittings to the new tram company on 8th May 1894. The price was more than £20,000, approximately £2.10s. for each £1 share, paid half in cash and half in shares of the tramway. In addition a sum of £75.17s.7d per annum was guaranteed until the tram was in operation, representing the average profit for the last five years. The new company continued to run the buses until their tramway was opened. All employees were retained by the new company, one well-known character 'Bus Jamie' (James Robertson) continuing with Perth Corporation as tram driver number 1. The bus manager, John Emslie, who had been with the company since 1884, went on to run the corporation's horse and electric trams initially.

Above: Lower Scone, probably in the 1880s with the laden bus collecting passengers outside the Scone Arms public house. For 21 years from 1863 the bus linked the village to Perth Station, usually running six times daily. On market days it was extended to Balbeggie. Most shareholders were local people who eventually received regular 4% returns, then were well recompensed when it was sold to the Tram Company.

All in all, the Omnibus Company provided a valuable, if unspectacular, service and in the end gave a good return to its shareholders. The stables at the top end of New Scone were enlarged to accommodate the additional tram horses, and stood until the site was reconstructed for the electric trams. The old bus company was wound up in December 1903.

During the period under consideration Perthshire was the fourth largest (in area) of all Scotland's administrative authorities. In addition to the landward area of the county, it contained several large Burghs given an independent status which sustained their individuality and kept them – and their rate income – outwith the jurisdiction of the county officials. In this book only road transport services which originated in or served the City of Perth are under consideration, serving the immediately surrounding catchment area. The development of public road vehicular transport in and around these Burghs (Blairgowrie for example) is for another book. The title 'City' is one to which the citizens of Perth were (and are) accustomed to use historically, but has only been officially granted for use since 14th March 2012 when it won a contest for the title in a UK-wide competition held to commemorate the Diamond Jubilee of Queen Elizabeth. Official recognition – if such a thing can truly exist in this context – was 'removed' in 1975 during local government reorganisation, a decision much resented by inhabitants of the 'Fair City'. This title was used by Sir Walter Scott in his 1828 novel *The Fair Maid of Perth* and the common description of Perth as a city most probably came from its status as an 'ecclesiastical city' with St. John's Kirk dating back to about 1440, although there was a much earlier Christian place of worship on this site. The place had first been known as St. John's Toun, this reflected today in the title of the local football club. Legally Perth had the status of a town, although all the necessary qualifications for city designation were in place, and changed little with the 1975 fiasco – road and other 'official' signage did not change, retaining the use of the long-standing 'city' description during these 37 dispossessed years.

Above: Generally the bus started its run from Kinnear's Inn at the top (north) end of the village, where it is seen in this 19th century photograph. Although by the 1870s already known as Kinnear's, the licensee for some years was John Robertson, possibly father of 'Jeems' the bus driver. Note the boy conductor with bugle for alerting potential travelers before departure. For a time known as the 'Aerodrome' the pub then had a spell as a Chinese restaurant, but has now reverted to its age-old appellation.

Above: The Omnibus Company's stables at the top of Scone's main street, just before the junction with Mansfield Road. The site was taken over and used by the horse tramway company, with the open shed used for car storage and the stables, on the left, augmented by a new block to the right. With hindsight, it would have been a much more practical plan to build a new central depot for the electric trams, but this was never proposed by the Westminster-based engineers who supervised the reconstruction.

Perth and District Tramways Company Limited (1892-1903)

Proposals for replacing the bus service by trams were heard intermittently from 1881, not long after bus operations began to show a profit. However it was not until ten years later, in November 1891, that a letter was sent to the local authority proposing this. The nascent company obtained advice from Wm Allan Carter CE, who had tramway experience in both Edinburgh and Aberdeen. He advised use of a track gauge of 3 ft 6 ins to minimise street widenings. Perth Bridge was considered problematic, particularly since mechanical power operation was still under consideration. He advised "…the use of mechanical power … is a source of anxiety … because an accident there caused by frightened horses could only have a very fatal result.' [sic] It was proposed to lay a single track across the bridge, to one side, but any perceived problem was overcome by laying double track for the length of the bridge.

In March 1892 these ideas crystallised with issue of a prospectus for the tramway. Interestingly, the intention was to use electric power, and the directors of the (very soon fully subscribed) youthful company visited undertakings where accumulator power was in use. In January 1893 an Austrian, Ludwig Epstein, gave a lecture in Scone Hall on 'Electric Traction' – a clear indication of intent. His company, the Epstein Electric Accumulator Company, was in process of equipping six cars for the Birmingham Central Tramway and the local directors went to observe the system in operation. Unfortunately this was not an unqualified success, although it was in use for two years and the idea of accumulator use in Perth at this stage was shelved. When eventually horse cars were purchased, it was stated that they were suitable for accumulator powered use. In preparation of estimates, it was considered that the rolling-stock necessary would be just five cars; two small double deck, one single deck, and two for workmen, plus only ten horses.

Above: Car 3 in original condition, before lengthening in 1899, at the terminus outside the depot in Scone. The driver is the redoubtable John Bruce, conductor Tom Inglis, and horses Sharp and Jean – from John's prodigious memory. The unmade state of the roadway is typical of those days.

With a rapid take-up of shares (the offer fully subscribed by December), the new Company moved promptly to put its plans into effect. Following agreement with the two local authorities involved, the city and the county, the contract for track construction was let to Alex Brunton & Sons. Perhaps they had an advantage, as the whinstone paving setts came from their quarry at Inverkeithing. Ground was broken in County Place on 28th May 1895, anticipating track laying would be completed in three months, but actually took four. On 10th September the line was inspected for the Board of Trade prior to opening for public use with Major Marindin RE travelling over the 3 mile line, finding that it was in fit condition for use. The rails (79 lb/yd) were laid as single track from end to end, with just four passing places, plus double track over Perth Bridge. Marindin required that a passing place be added near the terminus in Glasgow Road, and over time additional loops were added as found necessary.

Drivers were instructed by David MacDonald, an experienced driver from Dundee tramways, with all in order by the 17th for the opening ceremony to take place. Three cars decorated with flags took officials and guests to a cake and wine reception in Scone Public Hall, the first car driven by Mr W S Ferguson, the Company Chairman – as a farmer he would have no difficulty with such a task. The initial frequency was a car every half-hour, soon found to be inadequate. At the Annual Meeting – the fourth – a dividend was declared of 2%, the results of operating the bus prior to the tramway opening. Four small cars were obtained, said to be suitable for use with oil motors if desired while a fifth car was an open 'toastrack' for workmen's services. From May 1896 staff were issued with uniforms of 'claret colour with scarlet facings'.

After a year, it was proposed to build extensions to Craigie, Cherrybank and Dunkeld Road, with the first, to Craigie duly opening on 1st April 1898. The Cherrybank line followed, opened on 1st October, and for the trip of just over 3½ miles 40 minutes was allowed. A short siding at the east end of the High Street was added at the start of 1898 which became the terminus for the Craigie car – the route generally run by one car. Four additional larger (42-seat) cars were purchased, the first arriving in July 1896. At the beginning of 1899 the original 24-seat vehicles were rebuilt to carry 40 passengers, by J T Keiller of York Place. It had been intended that the small cars would be pulled by a single horse, but this proved impossible. The experience with the large cars convinced the directors that the two horses found necessary would be better employed hauling larger vehicles and thus more passengers. A trial of two Canadian mules was not a success.

An 1890s Scone scene with a small flock of sheep being driven up Perth Road. The only road vehicle is the tram waiting by the depot to begin its journey into Perth and on to the Station or, later, to Cherrybank.

Throughout its short existence the company proved financially stable and returned a regular dividend, generally in the order of 4%, indicating that it was being run economically by the manager George Castle, formerly of the Edinburgh Tramway Company. According to the Annual Reports the Company carried about one million passengers each year, but this appears to have been derived from the total number of tickets issued. However, the lines were divided into non-overlapping 1d stages, for which separate tickets were issued; thus a passenger travelling from Scone to the Station would pass through three such 1d stages and been counted as three passengers! The twice-weekly Balbeggie bus was run by John Campbell, the Scone cab proprietor, who continued to keep his bus in the car shed.

At the end of 1899 the Company proposed to electrify their lines, and promoted a Provisional Order to allow mechanical or electrical power. This galvanised the Corporation into action, particularly since a municipal power station was at the planning stage, which was intended to include capacity for tramways. The company valued their assets at £30,000; the initial offer from the Corporation was £20,000, so a degree of compromise was necessary; an assessment by Jas Moore CE produced a figure of £22,965. After the Corporation's initial offer was rejected, following negotiation, agreement on a purchase price of £21,800 was reached. The date of handover was agreed as 15th March 1903, the Company's shareholders receiving 20/- in the £1. The horse tramway had served the community well for its short existence, but this was not the end of the matter. The Corporation had the right to acquire the undertaking, but until its Provisional Order was enacted, it did not have authority to operate. It was thus necessary to agree with the Company's directors for them to manage and run affairs until such time as the Order received Royal Assent. While there had been several objections to the Order, these were all ultimately withdrawn and arrangements rapidly concluded for transfer of books and assets. This took place formally on 7th October according to the Council Minutes, but a week later according to the contemporary press report. In reality, the Company worked the lines for the Corporation until the last car on Saturday 10th, the Corporation operating from the first car on Monday 12th, there being no Sunday service. That same month all eight ordinary cars were 'painted, gilded, lined and varnished' for the new owners by W R Smith, painter and decorator of Bridgend, the workmen's car only 'part painted and lettered on both sides'. Perth Corporation's coat of arms replaced that of the County, which had been carried previously.

Horse cars – all passed to the Corporation:

1	Double deck, garden seats, seating 12/12, Brown, Marshall 1895 *
2	Double deck, garden seats, seating 12/12, Brown, Marshall 1895 *
3	Double deck, garden seats, seating 12/12, Brown, Marshall 1895 *
4	Double deck, garden seats, seating 12/12, Brown, Marshall 1895 *
5	Single deck, toastrack, seating 35, Britannia Rly Carriage Works 1895†
6	Double deck, garden seats, seating 22/18, Midland Rly Carriage Works 1896
7	Double deck, garden seats, seating 22/18, Midland Rly Carriage Works 1897
8	Double deck, garden seats, seating 22/18, Midland Rly Carriage Works 1897
9	Double deck, garden seats, seating 22/18, Midland Rly Carriage Works 1902

*   Cars extended to seat 20/18 by J T Keiller of Perth 1899 (22/18 also stated)
†   Converted to water tank trailer 1908

Looking north at the tram terminus with the prominent red Dumfriesshire sandstone tower of the 'New' – 1887 – Church of Scotland dominating the horizon at what was then the north end of the village. A car lettered for the Craigie route is poking out of the depot. Originally with two tracks, it was extended by a third track to accommodate all nine cars.

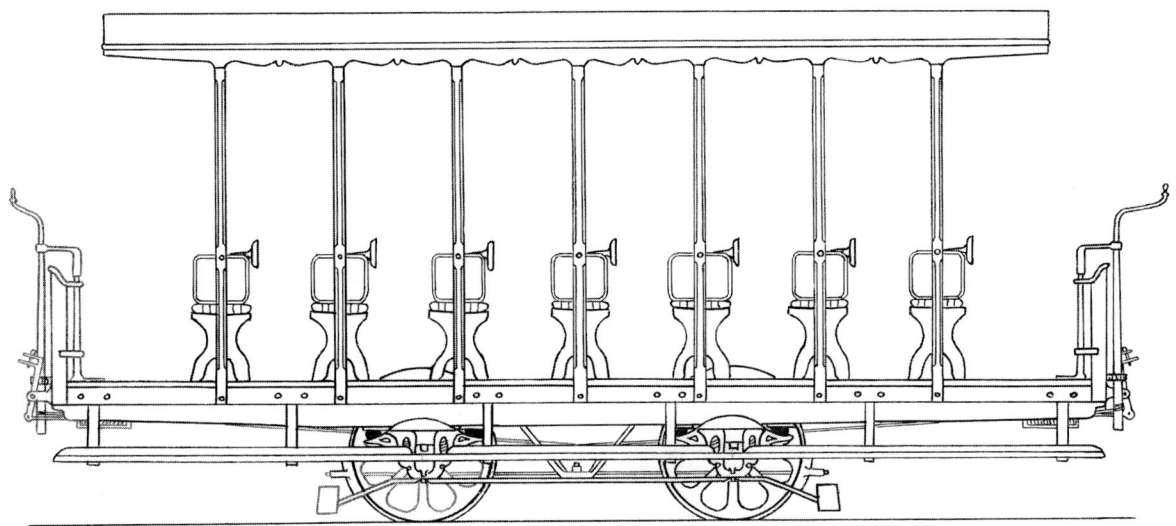

Of the original fleet of just five cars, number 5 was unique – a single-deck 'toastrack' for 35 passengers intended for use on workmen's services. Strangely perhaps, there is no record of its use on summer days, when it could have been appreciated. No photograph has come to light, but a contemporary drawing shows its appearance.

Lower Scone at the turn of the 20th century, with one of the then-new larger cars heading in to Perth, the view photographed from what was to become the site of Scone's War Memorial. The old stone houses bordering Perth Road have gone, demolished c1960 to be replaced by four single storey homes for elderly residents.

One of the original cars making the turn from High Street to George Street. These were said to be the smallest tramcars in Scotland and it had been the intention to use one horse to pull them. Unfortunately the haul up to the Old Bridge with a laden car proved too heavy a load, so two animals were necessary. With the benefits lost, the cars were lengthened and became more economical to operate.

(From the collection of A Findlay)

The middle of Perth's High Street is obviously just the spot for a tête-á-tête; there is little chance of the horse tram, paused by the Post Office, causing any interruption. At the far end of the street is the spire of the B-listed St Paul's Church which dates to 1807. After closure in 1984 its fabric was allowed to deteriorate until it was placed on the 'Buildings at risk' register while varied plans for re-use were debated and discarded. Work has now commenced to refurbish this critical city-centre venue as a 'versatile public space' with initial work to make the structure safe.

Well-patronised horse trams pause on the passing place on Perth's High Street by the grand Post Office building. It could be said that the height of the structure was out of scale with the rest of the architecture, but it certainly 'made a statement'. It opened to the public at the end of June 1898, built from Cullaloe quarry, Fife, sandstone, which is said to be the closest to the Craigleith stone which was used for most of Edinburgh's New Town. This photograph can be dated with a fair degree of accuracy to 1898 or 1899.

Since the frequency of the horse trams was generally every 20 minutes it becomes apparent that the photographer in many cases waited until one was present to add to the composition. There were others, of course, who would wait until the pesky moving object had cleared off out of their scene. Looking east along the High Street this photo shows the tram track making a right-angled turn into South Methven Street, reflecting the grid pattern of many main streets in the city centre.

The next such 90° bend took the tram from South Methven Street into County Place at South Street Port. The driver is clad for the summer with a boater straw hat, while the young lad conductor is boarding at the rear step. This is one of the later, slightly larger cars, which had longer platforms divided by a brass pole. Original cars 1 to 4, when lengthened, did not have this convenient feature. The smartly turned-out postie appears to be deep in thought.

The Craigie branch was the only addition – other than the extension to Cherrybank, but it tapped a new district, and again we have to be grateful to the photographer for waiting for the horse tram to complete the composition. The terminus for this line was at the far end of Priory Place, at Queen Street, at the end on the right. The scene is instantly recognisable, with little change. However, the air is fresher now; then the North British Railway's engine shed was just behind the shops, the air often thick with smoke.

Car 9 was the final purchase and ran for just three years. At Cherrybank terminus on Glasgow Road at the junction of Main Street and Low Road. Cherrybank school is on the right. The extended tram line was single track for its entire length; presumably when planned there was no consideration of a frequent service.

Perth Corporation Tramways
(horse and petrol operations 1903–05)

On 15th March 1903 Perth Council took over the local tramway company as a going concern, but day to day operation was provided by the directors and staff until mid-October. The eight drivers and seven conductors were decked out in new grey uniforms with red piping, while the two inspectors got navy blue frock coats and caps with gold braid – all very imposing and suitable for their new role as municipal employees. A frosty winter's morning in December saw what was recorded as Perth's first self-propelled tram "…on the hill to Cherrybank terminus the horses stumbled to a halt, unable to find a grip on the slippery setts; the driver grasped the situation, unhitched the team and allowed the car – including its passengers – to freewheel all the way back downhill as far as Rose Crescent. The horses were cautiously led down by the conductor, without their burden, rehitched and proceeded onwards in the approved fashion". Winter overcrowding was rife – that same December the Craigie car was stopped in pouring rain and a head count revealed no less than 38 passengers inside and on the platforms, plus a few drenched souls on the outside seats.

After hearing submissions from several firms of consulting engineers, the Council in their wisdom decided to discontinue the services of Wm Allan Carter of Edinburgh, but to take advice on electrification from Messrs Kincaid, Waller, Manville, & Dawson of Westminster [KWMD], who "would be able to do the work in a modern manner". This change was not received well in some quarters, particularly since Carter was involved with a similar but larger scheme for Leith and knew the area well. The question was already being asked, '…are Perth Council to well- or ill-manage or bungle their new acquisition?' The seeds of doubt were already being sown.

John Lambert, Burgh Electrical Engineer, who had been involved in design of the new power plant to supply the tramways, was given the additional role of Tramways Manager.

In addition to the generating plant, the Council had also incurred costs to raise the specification of the new Victoria Bridge to make it adequate for electric trams. It had been contemplated that in time tracks would be laid on South Street, over this new bridge, and round to Bridgend, but this never materialised. The Old Bridge was deemed adequate for trams – after all, it had for years successfully carried 15 ton steam rollers. As it was intended that the horse trams would be run during the reconstruction period, and since their depot at Scone was to be rebuilt for the new trams, a temporary facility for the horse cars was needed. This was built on the site of an old reservoir, at the city boundary and had three open-air tracks on sleepers filled between with ash. Temporary timber stables were also provided, the spot later known as the "cuddies' grave", even now not built on although surrounded on three sides by Gannochy bungalows..

KWMD produced a preliminary report which brought into play factors not previously considered; they had discovered that concrete below the horse line was at best only 4 inches thick and would have to be replaced. At this precise time a correspondent to a local paper put forward the suggestion that a 'petrol motor' service could be substituted, but Mr Dawson of KWMD was strongly against such an idea. However at the beginning of March the Council's Treasurer Laurie paid a visit to the 'Granton Tramway Company', where Mr Stirling showed him an experimental petrol engined tramcar. This, he explained, could operate on existing tracks, avoiding reconstruction costs, and required no expensive overhead or feeders. This had obvious financial benefit, and was of great interest, so much so that a Council delegation was sent to inspect it.

What the group saw in Granton was a relic of Edinburgh's horse tramway, fitted with a 9 horse power Stirling petrol engine, running on a short standard gauge track behind the factory. This building – which still stands [2018] – is the oldest purpose-built motor manufactory in Britain, dating from 1898. The deputation were suitably impressed, and although the cost comparisons were soon shown to be misleading, they agreed that Stirling should supply a 16 hp petrol tram for trial in Perth. In Stirling's opinion the tracks in Perth were suitable for further ten years use by light cars. Stirling requested 150 guineas for this experiment. The Corporation offered £100, subject to the car being in Perth within two months, i.e. by the end of May. It was to be proved by running faultlessly for at least 100 miles before acceptance.

This was an impossibly tight time-scale, and Stirling was let down by the builder of the tramcar body (thought to be G F Milnes of Hadley in Shropshire). At the end of May this date had to be extended to the end of June … then to the end of July; all the while the patience of the Council was wearing thin. It was confidently reported in the local press that the car had, in fact, arrived in the town on 5th July, but this proved an illusion; it was also said that the car had been retained so that it could be inspected by Leith's Councilors, but this cut no ice with their counterparts in Perth. Eventually when it did arrive (on 21st July) the various parts which had been removed for the rail journey were refitted in the street outside Bailie Keillor's garage in York Place. It was placed on the rails there after midnight, but further two hours were spent in preparation before it set off, exploding detonators on the rails as it progressed, until it got to Perth Bridge where it came to a standstill on the approach grade. It reversed and ran to St. Leonard's Bridge, where it again reversed and came through the town and on to Scone – leaving the track on just two occasions. Some further late-night forays followed, but the car was returned to Granton for a new radiator. Why the original temporary radiator could not be replaced in Perth was not answered. On 9th August the frustrated Councillors advised that should it not be operable within two weeks the contract would be abrogated. The car reappeared on the day the ultimatum expired, and while the Stirling Company maintained that they had fulfilled their obligations, the Council disagreed. In their opinion the trial had failed since 'the vehicle had refused to keep to the rails' which was countered by Stirling's assertion that the rails and particularly the points were defective. On 1st September it was announced that a larger engine was to be fitted and the tram was removed for three weeks – not to Granton on this occasion – but to a shed in the NBR goods yard. On 20th September it reappeared, with a new 26.4 horse power engine. On the night of 21st September it travelled relatively successfully over the system and was presented for official inspection on the 29th. With some 57 passengers (initially) it left the Cross, travelled successfully to Scone and back, but then disgraced itself by spectacularly derailing in Bridgend when the bend approaching the bridge was taken at excessive speed. It ended up against the front of Miss Laing's fruiters shop and was only rerailed with difficulty. It proceeded on its way, now with a distinctly lesser number of passengers. The following day the Council voted by 13 votes to 3 to waste no more time and totally abandon the petrol tram experiment forthwith. Complaint was also raised regarding the ever present smell of petrol, and the loud noise of the engine when 'ticking-over'. In mid October the car was quietly returned to Granton, with a report suggesting it had been sold; 'The Petrol Puffer has been consigned to the policies of Wemyss Castle in Fife where it is used for conveying visitors through the Grounds'. Mr R G E Wemyss of Wemyss Castle was then planning a 7 mile tramway (of 3 ft 6 ins gauge coincidentally) to link Kirkcaldy and Leven. Nothing has been uncovered of any subsequent use of the vehicle, a double deck car with three window saloon, seating 22 out and 18 inside.

In the meantime, Perth Council – perhaps anticipating how the petrol tram experiment would end – had arranged for tenders to be advertised for the contracts for electrification of their tramways. They were thus in a good position to act promptly following the petrol tram distraction. On KWMDs advice tenders were accepted, from R W Blackwell & Co for the track and overhead, from Callander's Cable Co for power supply and feeders, and from Hurst Nelson & Co for twelve cars. Power was to be obtained from the Council's power station at the Shore which had been inaugurated on 1st June 1901. On 17th January 1905 Callanders started work, the intention being to have work complete by May. Again circumstances conspired to prevent this; a ship carrying Norwegian setts foundered en route and rails, from the Middleborough Steel Co, were delayed. Added to this, poor weather affected progress. When work reached the High Street a labour force of over 450 men was employed to speed completion. These contracts brought much-needed work – albeit of a temporary nature – to the area.

During the construction period a horse car service, either using temporary track, or operating on either side of the works was attempted. The oft-debated extension to Dunkeld Road was built at this time, bringing the little system to its final extent, amounting to just under five route miles. On the first day of electric service horse car operation ceased at 2.30 pm, the cars running finally into the temporary depot. Here they languished until mid November when the entire effects of the horse tram operation were auctioned off, including the horses – but not the vehicles. At the sale even the temporary buildings were sold (for £83.15.3d) then quickly dismantled, the site being restored with soon no evidence of its temporary use. Horses and harness raised £564.19.7d, the sale making £1137.12.3d in total. Three cars were taken to the Burgh yard at Craigiehaugh where they were refurbished for use as passenger shelters at the termini at Scone, Craigie and Dunkeld Road; that at Scone was fondly remembered for its impromptu concerts. The toastrack was stripped of its seats and fitted with a water tank, and towed by an electric car to 'lay the dust' when required. The other five redundant horse cars were taken to the Surveyor's yard at Craigiehaugh to be sold; the last two went in 1910.

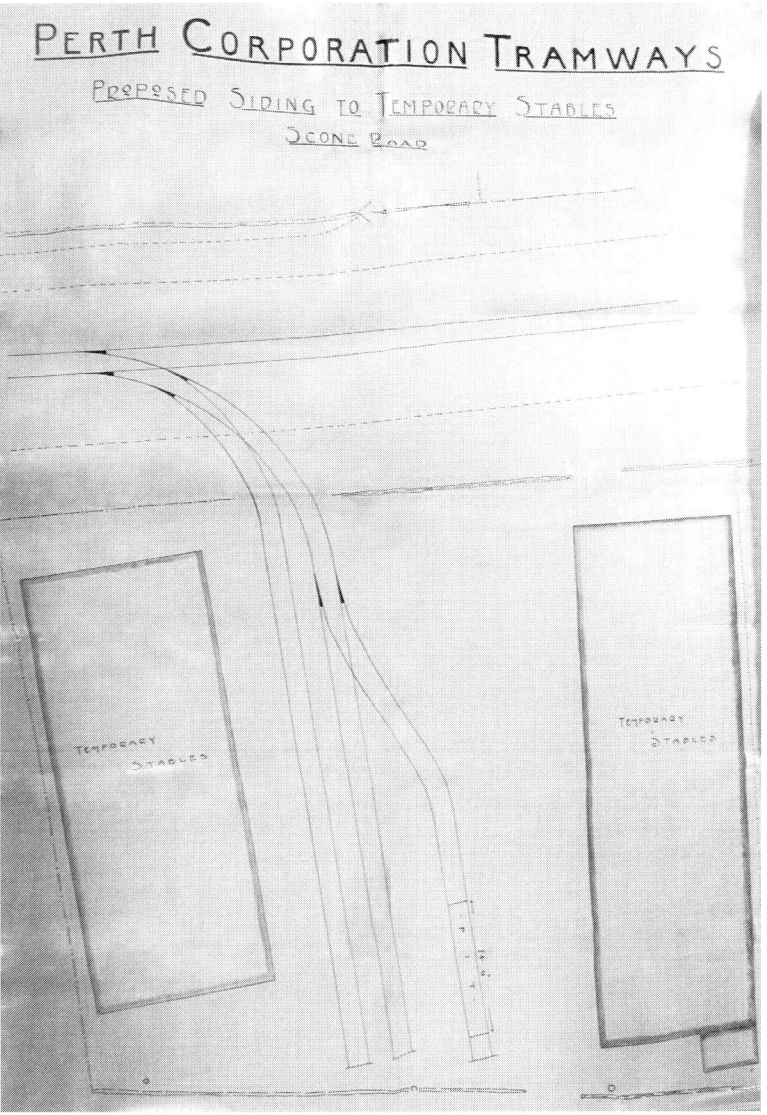

Right: Reproduced from an old plan for the temporary depot at 'Cuddie's Grave'. The site is still identifiable on the east side of the road to New Scone, as a well maintained small park. It is shown as parcel number 737 on the Ordnance Survey 25 inch plans.

(Image courtesy CulturePK.)

The Perth and District Tramways Company, Limited.

PAY SHEET.

For Week ending 7th November 1903.

Name	Role	Total	Extra	Rate			Signature
Jas. Emslie	Manager	6		34/	1	14 .	J. Emslie
W. G. Snell	Inspector	6		27/6	1	7 6	W. Snell
J. Thomson	"	6		22/	1	2 .	Jas Thomson
J. Robertson	Driver	6		21/	1	1 .	J. Robertson
J. Bruce	"	6		21/	1	1 .	J. Bruce
W. Wanliss	"	6		21/	1	1 .	W. Wanliss
D. Beveridge	"	6		21/	1	1 .	D. Beveridge
J. Brown	"	6		21/	1	1 .	J. Brown
D. Wanliss	"	6		20/	1	. .	D. Wanliss
J. Angus	"	6		20/	1	. .	J. Angus
J. Fowler	Spare Driver	6		18/	.	18 .	J. Fowler
J. Baxter	Conductor	6		14/	.	14 .	Wm Baxter
L. Marshall	"	6		12/	.	12 .	Lawrence Marshall
W. Brown	"	6	1/	10/	.	11 .	W. Brown
J. Cochrane	"	5½		13/	.	11 11	J. Cochrane
D. Beveridge	"	6		13/	.	13 .	D. Beveridge
P. Stevenson	"	6		13/	.	13 .	P. Stevenson
J. McPherson	"	6		9/	.	9 .	J. McPherson
J. Stewart	"	6		18/	.	18 .	J. Stewart
G. Craigon	Spare & Washer	6		14/	.	14 .	George Craigon
P. Lalletty	Feeder	6		23/	1	3 .	P. Lalletty
J. Marshall	Strapper	6		19/	.	19 .	John MacKay
C. McKenzie	"	6		19/	.	19 .	J. Marshall
W. Scott	"	6		19/	.	19 .	W. Scott
J. Murray	"	6	3/	19/	1	2 .	J. Murray
J. Collins	Trace Boy	6		8/	.	8 .	+
J. Thomson	"	5		7/	.	5 10	J. Thomson
A. Harris	"	6		9/	.	9 .	A. Harris
				£	24	7 3	

Payroll sheet for 7th November 1903, immediately after acquisition by the Corporation. James Robertson ('Jeems') who came from the Omnibus Company is the first driver, followed by John Bruce. Wage rates are a reflection of the purchasing power of money then. A family could be raised well on a guinea a week. (Image courtesy CulturePK.)

A Fair City Favourite.

Photo by Mr A. T. Torrance, Perth.

"JEEMS."

Such a well-known local character was James 'Jeems' Robertson that he even featured on his own picture-postcard. Initially the Corporation issued cap badges with the employee number incorporated. Jeems was driver number 1, seen on his badge here.

The unfortunate petrol tram which, it was hoped, was to be the answer to Perth's transport conversion. It is seen at the makers workshop in Granton, by Edinburgh. It is reported to have ended its days at Wemyss Castle in Fife – but doing what? The laird of Wemyss, Randolph Wemyss was instrumental in building a tramway from Kirkcaldy to Leven which transformed the neighbourhood, and it is intriguing to think he might have planned for it to be personal transport.

IN AFFECTIONATE REMEMBRANCE OF

RING OUT THE OLD RING IN THE NEW

THEY DID THEIR WORK THEIR DAY IS DONE

THE PERTH HORSE CARS
WHICH SUCCUMBED TO AN ELECTRIC SHOCK ON TUESDAY OCTOBER 31ST 1905

A local publisher, J K Thompson, caught the mood of the time producing these 'In Memoriam' cards to mark the passing of the horse trams. Two of the redundant vehicles are seen passing on the High Street loop east of Scott Street.

Left: Advert selling all the effects of the horse tramway – except the cars. Everything one might need to run a horse tramway, but its days were past.

Below: Further use was in fact found for all the old disused tram cars. A pair ended at the Sanatorium, while others were used as shelters, including this one outside the new electric tram depot in Scone village with high Edwardian fashion in evidence. The sole remaining evidence of the trams here is one still standing left-hand gate pillar of this pair.

Opposite, upper: Track reconstruction was accomplished rapidly – there was then no consideration of any necessity to relocate any below ground services such as drains and water mains. There appears to be no attempt either to divert High Street traffic or provide dedicated pedestrian walkways. To be able to carry the work out in this manner ensured it was done rapidly, unlike events related to the new Edinburgh tramway!

Opposite, lower: Total occupation of the street at the foot of George Street. The track to the right leads to the short stub terminal used by cars for Craigie and Dunkeld Road. Instructions were issued that to avoid congestion no more than one car at a time was to use the terminus, and cars were not to obstruct George Street. During the upheaval a service of sorts was maintained by the horse cars, generally running on either side of the work in progress.

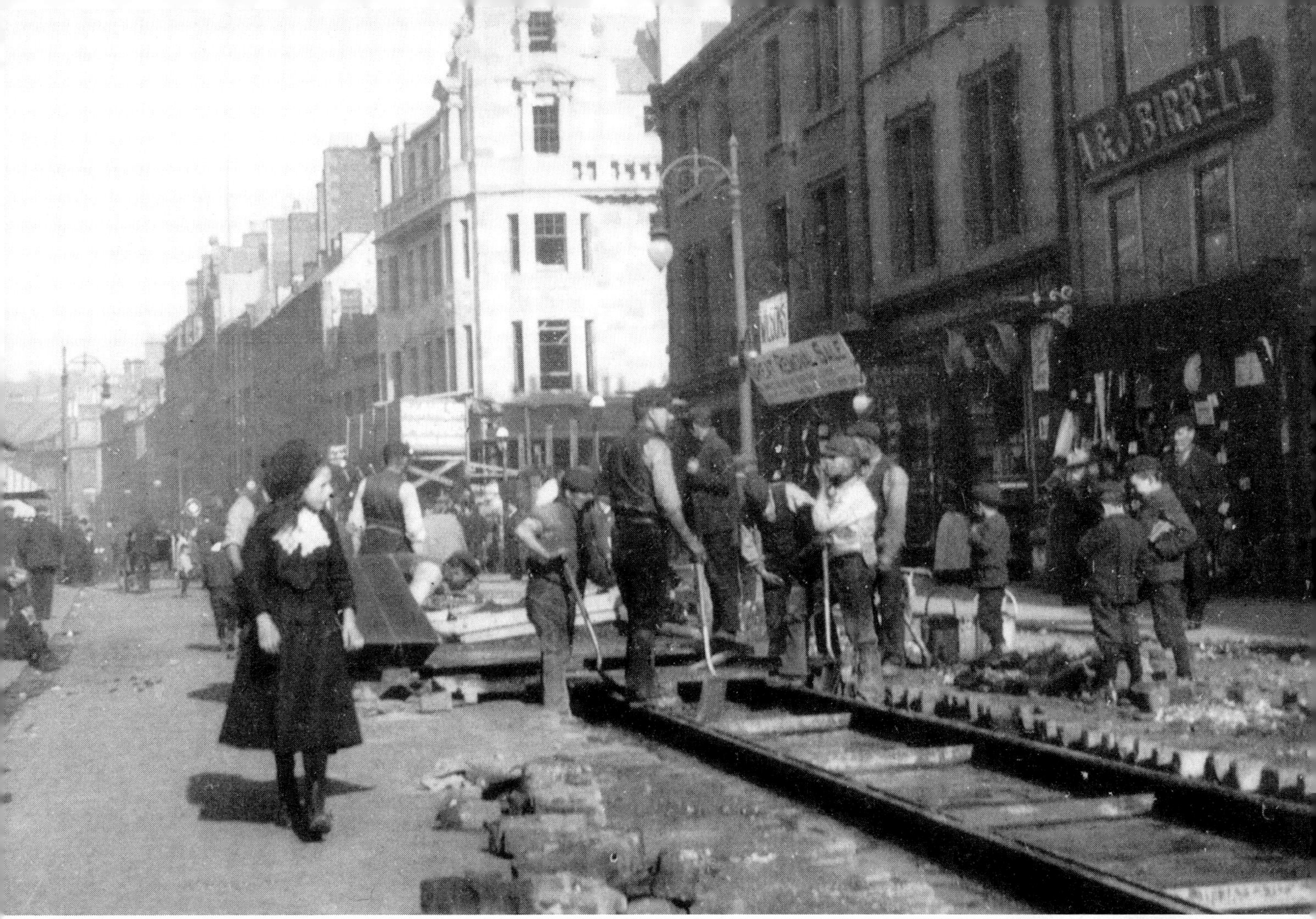
BIRRELL

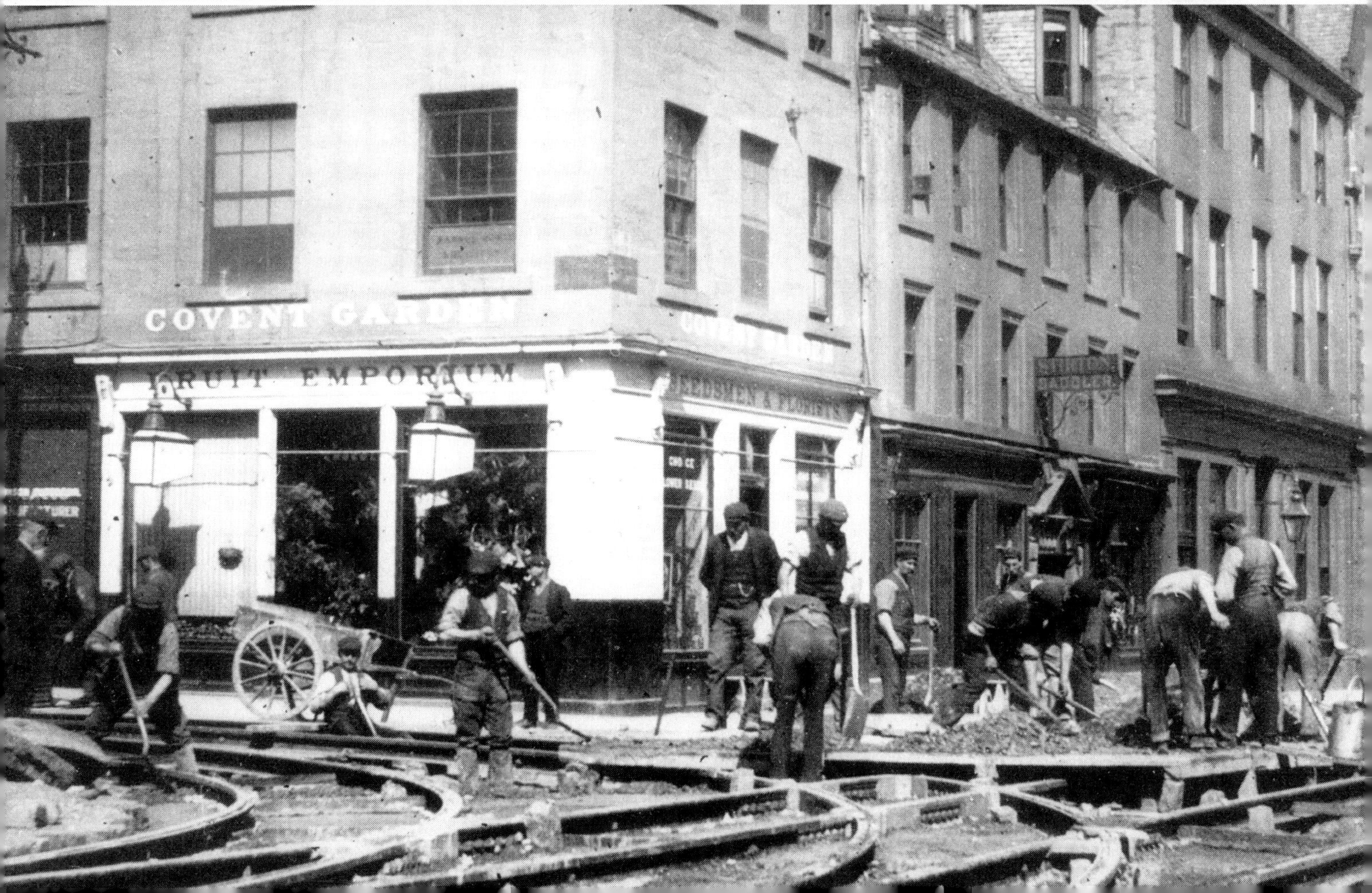
COVENT GARDEN
FRUIT EMPORIUM
COVENT GARDEN
SEEDSMEN & FLORISTS
SADDLER

Looking up South Methven Street with the junction under construction. The fancy cast iron base to the lighting pole carries the city coat of arms. Many of these could be seen along the former tram routes until well into the 1980s. As will be seen the space left for the concrete foundation below the rails was minimal and the Consulting Engineers reported that this was not satisfactory. After some years use joints loosened and repairs were necessary with the rail ends 'Thermit' welded together.

Relaying the setts was one of the final tasks and a specialised trade, usually paid at 'piece rate' by the measure rather than by the hour. With most streets in towns surfaced with durable whin or granite, the road surface was almost indestructible. It could be opened easily, but repairs – especially in later years – were often poorly executed, leading to complaint from pandered road users. Smooth tarmac which in many cases replaced the setts is also only good as long as it is well maintained. This is Glasgow Road at Rose Crescent; the original horse tram terminus.

The only extension to the system was a branch line up Dunkeld Road, seen under construction at Barrack Street – with the Black Watch barracks on the left. The proliferation of chimneys makes it appear that Perth was an industrialised city; these were from the Wallace jute works and Balhousie damask linen works, many of whose workers lived close by. This view is looking north up Dunkeld Road from St. Ninian's Cathedral corner.

Perth Corporation Tramways
(electric operation 1905–1929)

While contracts for track and overhead proceeded satisfactorily unfortunately the same cannot be said regarding that for the cars. Documents now available throw light on the changes and errors which nearly ended with the Council, their Consulting Engineers and Hurst Nelson resorting to the courts to resolve matters. While there were other issues, the most significant related to the height of the vehicles, as defined by the interior height of the saloon, determined by the Council as 6 ft 3 ins. Hurst Nelson's Order Book records an entry, on 21st October 1904, for "Twelve double deck electric cars, Westinghouse equipment, Hurst Nelson Brill-type trucks … Brecknell, Munro and Rogers folding steps." The height problem was a problem dictated by the railway bridge over King Street on the Craigie route which had clearance in the centre of just 15 ft 5 ins between the road surface and the underside of the arch.

What can be established from remaining correspondence is that the height to which the cars were to be built was altered by the Engineer, albeit with good reason, but without putting the matter to the Council for agreement beforehand. The approved specification indicated the internal floor to ceiling height to be 6 ft 3 ins, despite Hurst

Nelson indicating then that the normal internal dimension was 6 ft 6 ins. However KWMD instructed the car builders that the inside dimension was to be 6 ft 1⅜ ins, this only arrived at after the King Street road surface was lowered by 3 inches, and special dispensation was obtained from the Board of Trade to accept a clearance from the top deck floor of the tram to the underside of the bridge at 6 ft 0 ins, where their stipulation was for 6 ft 6 ins. Unfortunately this was not explained to the Council prior to the instruction being given to Hurst Nelson. Perth Councilors appeared fixated regarding this dimension… "…this alteration will cause serious inconvenience to passengers in travelling inside the cars. It will be impossible for a man of average height with a tall hat to stand erect within any of the cars, and there will be constant liability to the hats of passengers being damaged by coming in contact with the roof. It is also thought that the low height of the cars as now completed will prejudice people of over average height availing themselves of the cars, and the Revenue would therefore suffer for a period of from fifteen to twenty years…". The Council took a legal opinion, considering that the cars (which had by now all been built to the dimension supplied by KWMD) should be altered to the originally required height, with all costs met by KWMD, also that they were fully entitled to refuse to accept the cars, and that the consequential costs of this should also be carried by the Engineers. Their legal opinion confirmed that the Engineers should have referred the matter to their clients, but that their liability would be limited to the cost of increasing to the specified height, or indeed to the recommended 6 ft 6 ins dimension.

It was considered that KWMD acted beyond their remit and their letter of explanation might appear to read as if the Council were being patronised…' it never occurred to us for one moment to consider that this was a matter in which a special report should be given to your Committee, as your Committee, with ourselves, would be ruled by an actual existing fact, and there was no point on which we conceived that we should take their instructions, as obviously, only one course was open, and the decision in a matter such as this we conceived to be entirely in our hands … had King Street Bridge been located on a route on which only a small percentage of the total cars would run, but such is not the fact. Of the 12 cars … one is provided as a spare and 11 are working cars, and of the 11 working cars we estimate that 6 cars will ordinarily have to pass under [the] Bridge, we think it would be unwise to have provided two types of cars … the proposal to increase the height of the whole of the cars at a heavy expenditure is one which you cannot legally carry out, as you will contravene the Regulations … if the Committee decide upon adopting this course, it will be absolutely against our advice, and we can take no responsibility whatever if the Committee see fit to act against our advice … we did not conceive it necessary to report this matter to the Committee, firstly, because the Committee would have been unable to in any way enable us to obtain the greater clearance and secondly … this is a matter in which we were entitled to exercise our best judgment and we can only regret that the Committee do not appreciate that we have acted to the best of our ability in their interests…' Philip Dawson (then junior partner of KWMD) went on to a distinguished career, was knighted, and served as a Member of Parliament.

Hurst Nelson were blameless, having acted on the engineers' instruction, but had, from their own point of view, attempted to vary the specification relating to the trucks and the steps, while the client changed the specification for the lifeguards. By the end of April 1905 six cars were ready for despatch (built to the low dimension) but construction of the new depot was not advanced sufficiently to accept them; indeed it was not until 12th August that the first three trucks were delivered. On 10th August an instruction was received to alter nine cars, increasing the inside height to 6 ft 6 ins, at a cost of £77.15.0d per car – a rise of nearly 25% on the bodywork cost of each. The first of these heightened cars, numbers 1 and 2, were despatched on 21st and 22nd September respectively, with a request that two unaltered cars were to be forwarded next; numbers 11 and 12 followed from Motherwell on 25th September. The others followed, 3 and 4 on 26th September, 6 on 28th, 5 and 7 on the 30th, then 8 and 9 two days later, leaving only number 10 – unaltered – at Hurst Nelson's works. The Council had instructed that 'Fisher' style lifeguards be substituted for the specified variety, at an additional cost of £4.10/- per car. This design was patented by Peter Fisher, manager of the Dundee tramways and was fitted to their cars but did not find much favour elsewhere.

The Board of Trade inspection was split, with overhead and electrical work examined by Major Trotter on 19th October, then the track and vehicles the following day by Lt Col von Donop. Needless to say after the fracas attending the King Street bridge clearances, this was given close scrutiny. The outcome was von Donop requiring that the low cars needed for use on the Craigie route, the only one which used this track, be painted a distinguishing colour. Cars 11 and 12, which had been delivered in the crimson lake colour scheme were repainted dark olive green at Scone Depot by Hurst Nelson employees. Car 10, still in Motherwell, was to be repainted green before delivery; the cost for repainting three cars and their trucks amounting to £31.5.0d

Above: One of the first trips by electric tram into town, at the beginning of October 1905, on Pitcullen Crescent, part of the main road leading to Scone and the north. The car had been delivered on 25th September and was fitted up for the Board of Trade inspection. As the inspector had to traverse the entire system including the Craigie branch which passed under the notorious low King Street Bridge it was necessary to use one of the low cars. Car 12 was later painted green along with its two companions, but at this time was in the standard crimson lake livery. One of the old horse cars follows at a discrete distance.

Mrs Love, wife of the Lord Provost drove the first car on the opening day, October 31st 1905. Earlier the old Scone bus had been brought out of retirement to transport the ladies of the official party to the power station where the tramway plant was started. The party returned to the Municipal Buildings where six cars were waiting which then traversed the complete system. Public service commenced at 2.30 pm when the horse cars were withdrawn, their place taken by the 'sparkies'. Routes were as run by the horse cars, plus Cross to Dunkeld Road. The trip from Scone to Cherrybank which had occupied 41 minutes was now accomplished in 25. In the evening, the company and guests were entertained to dinner by the engineers and contractors, but several Councilors boycotted this event, considering it wrong to accept hospitality from parties with whom they were still in dispute.

These disagreements between the Council, their engineers and Hurst Nelson festered and monies were kept back from their accounts. It was estimated that delays consequent on heightening the cars had incurred lost income during the summer period of £1,200. The folding steps fitted to the cars proved difficult to adjust, hence in August 1906 six were replaced by a Brush Company design which worked successfully elsewhere. Other cars were then fitted with replacements using a design patented by the Manager. £384 was retained from Hurst Nelson's account under this heading, also £400 from KWMD. Eventually a settlement was reached with £180 deducted from KWMD fees; but there was feeling that these disputes could have been avoided had the Council stayed with the local engineer, and that this was the price to be paid for supposedly more knowledgeable Westminster experts.

In September 1906 the Council received an enquiry from the National Electric & Construction Company offering to lease the town's tramways. This was dismissed out of hand; a decision that may have been hasty, and which was possibly later regretted. At this time, on the occasion of the local flower show, both Craigie and Dunkeld Road trams were extended to run through the town to Bridgend.

It was soon found that cars on the Craigie run were experiencing excessive wear on their brakes and Lambert proposed to fit track brakes to two cars. In October 1906 Hurst Nelson were instructed to fit their slipper brakes to the three low cars at a cost of £50 each. This was duly done, but as track deteriorated it was found that the brake shoes caught on misaligned rail joints, with unfortunate consequences. Those on cars 10 and 11 were removed, but car 12's lasted a little longer. This car also had, for a time, a drivers' windscreen, but this was found objectionable by drivers from the draughts created down the stairs – they preferred to be exposed to the elements. Much later, in October 1922, it was considered that all cars should have vestibule protection for platform staff, but this was abandoned as an unnecessary expense. Another idea, floated about this time suggested fitting all cars with top deck canvas covers, also not proceeded with.

Above: Car 11 was delivered with car 12 and they were used for driver familiarisation before the inspection. Drivers spent a few days in Dundee, being instructed there in the driving art before being let loose on the streets of Perth. Colonel von Donop undertook the inspection on 18th October, but it was not until 31st October that the horse cars were withdrawn and electricity took over. Car 11 is in the High Street at the Post Office and is lacking its destination box; it too was delivered painted crimson lake, but after von Donop's instruction at the inspection was repainted green at Scone Depot.

It was soon realised that the undertaking was not covering costs. In particular financing the debt incurred in purchase of the horse system and the cost of reconstruction was a heavy burden for the small system. An annual contribution of some £15,000 (or an annual addition of about 3d on the rates) was needed to serve this, and while trams operationally did not lose money, the bottom line showed a substantial deficit each year. The use of two cars on the short routes to Craigie and to Dunkeld Road to give a 15 minute frequency was uneconomic and it was realised that one car on each line could provide a 20 minute service. Each Councillor had ideas as to how economies could be made, including diverting the Dunkeld Road tram to serve the Station; the route became Cross–Dunkeld Rd–Station Entrance–Dunkeld Rd–Cross. This lasted just seven months from 1st October 1906. By March 1907 the Caledonian Railway had completed reconstruction of King Street bridge, increasing clearance by 1 ft 6 ins. The saga of tram height was over, but had this been undertaken two years earlier large lawyers' fees could have been avoided. The three low cars were now repainted crimson lake to match the others.

Above: Car 12 has attracted a number of interested bystanders on an early trip, but the spectacle was soon commonplace as the trams became an accepted feature of life. Also seen on the High Street at Kinnoull Street Post Office corner, the elaborate lamps showing the entrance to Perth Theatre. The learning period was not without incident – the trolley of one car left the wire in Pitcullen Crescent, damaging both trolley-pole and overhead support.

Lambert was instructed to report on the system during 1907 which highlighted some of the more obvious losses. A significant cost resulted from amount of dead mileage running cars to and from Scone Depot, the furthest point on the system, totalling nearly 300 miles a month. A central depot would have been much more economical, but this was never before suggested by KWMD or anybody else. The Scone site had developed from the bus company's stables, and use of that facility seemed a given; many employees then lived in Scone and that situation prevailed. Moving the home-ground of local football team St. Johnstone FC to a site closer to a tramline to generate traffic with sites at Crieff Road or near Fitzroy Terrace was suggested. From its formation, the club played at the Recreation Grounds at Craigiehaugh, off Edinburgh Road opposite the prison, just about as far from a tram route as possible. It was not until 1924 that St. Johnstone moved to Muirton Park on the north side of the city. Another proposition (not carried into effect) was to build a tourist tramway up Kinnoull Hill; the numbers of visitors to the 'Fair City' had fallen dramatically and this was a suggestion to entice them back. Lambert also suggested serving the short branch lines with one-man operated demi-cars, but the capital cost involved outweighed potential savings. Nobody, apparently, suggested converting two existing cars for this purpose. Some special fares were introduced in an attempt to lure passengers, with limited success. In addition to the three regular services, the Tramways Department had income from special cars after theatre performances and other similar functions. Mails were carried to sub-post offices and out to Scone, also producing a small contribution.

Above: Cars 1 and 2 were the next delivered, after having been altered by Hurst Nelson. The three cars accepted as built to the low height cost £234 10s each (excluding electrical equipment), the alterations not only introducing inherent structural weakness, but adding almost a third to the cost. Car 1 is seen outside Scone Depot, with traffic superintendent Mr Snell on the left with the bowler hat. This is probably the first service car to Cherrybank on 31st October 1905, a popular postcard by local photographer J K Thompson.

This scene was probably recorded in the spring or early summer of 1906, as the waiting room made from an old horse tram is outside the depot; this was authorised in February of that year. Car 5 has just set off from the terminus and has, on the top deck, a complement of top-hatted gentlemen – maybe a tad overdressed for your average tram passenger, but perhaps there is a meeting in town of the local funeral directors.

The annual market in the old village of Scone was once a significant event, but lost its importance when the village was removed to a 'planned' site on the Coupar Angus road, taking it away from Scone Palace approach. The event soon became little more than a children's funfair. Car 2 is making for the terminus having dropped off two ladies, in the summer of 1906.

A panorama across Lower Scone. The foreground cottages have gone now, opening a vista of Burnside behind. The Scone Arms, beside the electric tram, has in recent years had a chequered history. The nominal distinction between Old (original) Scone village and New (replacement) Scone was lost from 1997 when 'New' was dropped from the title – requiring replacement of road and other signs with the distinction.

Car 4 posed in the countryside between Scone and Perth, at Langley Cottages. This is a clear photo of this elusive car. While all were nominally used equally, 4 was remarkably camera shy. The louvres introduced when the saloon was heightened are apparent.

A windy day in Bridgend, on the east bank of the Tay, and at the end of John Smeaton's handsome 1771 bridge. Sir John Millais the noted pre-Raphelite and landscape artist declared that the view from the bridge across the North Inch to the distant Grampian mountains was the finest he had seen in all his travels. The assessment of the bridge's ability to carry the circa 8 tons trams was empirical to say the least – "15-ton steam rollers have been over it and it is still standing, so it will take the trams…". Car 1 is seen here, heading for Scone, also in 1906.

According to the information on this old postcard, it shows the goose 'Jock' making his daily perambulation from Bridgend and across Perth Bridge. Car 8, its conductor standing at attention, awaits the signal to proceed from the local 'Bobby'.

The Bridgend landfall of the bridge with the former toll house on the right. When built, a toll was extracted to pay for the bridge and its upkeep, with the right to collect tolls being let annually by roup. Until fairly recently a replica board gave indication of the old tolls, and there remains a similar board of regulations for (road) locomotives – traction engines – crossing. The beasts being walked over in charge of the lad on the left are probably from Perth Market, walking the purchase home being normal before motorised cattle floats.

One consideration was that the tramway was actually too small to operate beneficially, and extensions were mooted. Parliamentary authority was achieved in 1908 (at considerable legal cost) for four extensions; from Dunkeld Road along the Crieff Road to Unity Terrace, from Craigie to Craigie Burn, from High Street Port to Jeanfield Road, and down King Edward Street to the site of a potential central depot. The only track change was construction of an 80 yard single line extension from the Craigie terminus taking the track down to Windsor Terrace. As road traffic increased trams standing at Craigie were again considered to be an obstruction so in October 1924 the terminus was moved 20 yards back closer to Queen Street. At the same time, and for the same reason, the terminus at Dunkeld Road was moved back – by 3 yards! The Order of 1908 also included, significantly, 'power to operate omnibuses within the Burgh, and also in connection with the tramways beyond the Burgh for a distance not exceeding three miles from any part of the tramways'. The short extension at Craigie brought the tramways to a maximum length of 5 miles plus 22 yards.

As if to prove that spending more money would reduce costs, the Council two years later commissioned a report on their tramway from Peter Fisher, the highly experienced manager of Dundee's trams. In most respects he concurred with Lambert, but one of his main criticisms related to over-staffing; the total employed by the Tramways Department being 48, excluding the manager, no less than twelve at the Scone depot – allowing one per car. Three washers and three shedmen, a full-time painter and a full-time blacksmith were included. He considered that four posts here were superfluous, that only one inspector was required not two, and that boys employed for signalling at blind corners or junctions should be replaced by signalling apparatus. He found that the charge for power was higher than average and also examined the costs against savings resulting from construction of a central depot in King Edward Street. His conclusion was that, while it was unfortunate that this had not been done in 1905, the building and finance costs proved (by £140 per annum) to retain the existing arrangements. He examined the proposed extensions and concluded that none would repay the cost, or contribute anything to reduce losses. The befits of Sunday operation were obvious, but this was a matter for the ratepayers and their consciences; there had never been operation on the Sabbath in Perth. He concluded that – as was patently obvious – the tramway finances were in a bad way and the number of passengers per car mile was low. He concluded '…with careful handling, so that the best may be made of the business, the case is far from a hopeless one…' and offered his services to advise. Of his considerations, one small change was the introduction, from 3rd April 1910 of a limited Sunday operation. At this time the double track in the High Street was lengthened 100 yards eastwards from Meal Vennel to King Edward Street.

Advantage of the bus operating powers was taken from the first week of May 1911 (probably on Monday 1st) when a hired charabanc was used to operate to Almondbank village. However, complaints rapidly followed when it was taken off the regular – if infrequent – service to be used for hires and outings. Its usefulness was indisputable, the Council within a couple of months deciding to purchase a bus of their own. This proved to be the start of over two decades of bus operation by the Council. A consequence of Fisher's report was the removal of tramway management from Lambert's remit. He returned to his post as manager of the Burgh's expanding electrical power department, while W G Snell, erstwhile Traffic Superintendent, became interim Manager for three months, which was then ratified.

A feature of the tramways was the appearance of the illuminated car, or decorated cars. After the opening day, when a brightly-lit car toured the system after dark with the Corporation band playing on the top deck, it appeared to celebrate such occasions as the annual flower show, and for the 1911 Coronation of King George V, all cars running were decorated. Perhaps the decorated car should have been used to celebrate the news that at last the trams were running at a profit – assisted by income from the new bus service. From this point until 1917 was the only time when the trams did not require to be subsidised from the rates.

The Great War of 1914-18 created problems for the Perth transport system, as it did throughout the entire country, with able-bodied men called to arms. War industries brought an influx of traffic, but this evaporated rapidly after the Armistice. It was not until the middle of 1918 that it was found necessary to employ 'female conductors', then as men were demobilised they returned to their former positions and the girl conductors were deposed. After the war costs rose rapidly and a round of fare increases implemented from August 1918 unfortunately did not reverse decreasing passenger numbers. Decorated cars ran to celebrate the cessation of hostilities.

Track maintenance had suffered during the war, with the consequent necessity for heavy expenditure to bring track and cars back to proper state. The Council decided in June 1919, to purchase two new trams, and thus allow the existing cars to be withdrawn for very necessary overhaul. The legacy of the 'heightening exercise' when the cars were altered before having run a mile in Perth was inherent weakness in the basic structure. To overcome this, bracing and metal corner brackets were fitted which did help to stiffen the bodywork to limited degree. Panels were fitted under the stairs which, it was said, gave a corner for smokers on wet days. Offers were received from three companies for two new cars and that of the English Electric Company was accepted. When it was discovered that the Board of Trade could not authorise borrowing for new cars, the Committee decided to get one car, to be purchased from the reserve fund. When English Electric were advised, it was quickly made clear that the price quoted was for two cars and that the cost of one non-standard car would not be simply be half the price of two. They proposed instead that Perth take a standard design car. This did not suit the Council and there the matter was dropped, which was, with the benefit of hindsight, perhaps the best outcome. Significant change lay around the corner, and one new tram was not going to make the necessary difference to profitability.

Maintenance of the track and the width of roadway occupied by it was passed to the Burgh Surveyor's Dept, and in 1925 rail joints throughout – with the exception of Dunkeld Road – were welded, in a belated attempt to improve running. The miners' strike of 1921 saw curtailment of services to save power while the 1926 General Strike saw a few men trying to maintain a basic service. As a measure of gratitude the driver and conductor of the Craigie car received a gold albert, a pendant and 'a small canteen of cutlery' while their counterparts on the Dunkeld Road car each received a cheque from regular passengers. Platform staff often worked the same shifts for lengthy periods and knew the needs of their regulars – waiting for anyone delayed, making sure they got to work or school.

The heavy cost of track upkeep was causing increasing concern, with the Tramways Committee in December 1925 proposing that authority be obtained to borrow the funds. This was not accepted by the full Council; instead the Electrical Engineer, the Burgh Surveyor, the City Chamberlain and the Tramway Manager were all asked to produce reports. After consideration of these, further opinion was sought, this time from R Stuart Pilcher, manager of Edinburgh's Transport Department, who was regarded with good reason as one of the leading authorities of the day. He had not long earlier overseen the transformation of Edinburgh's out-dated cable-operated trams into a modern electric system in a remarkably short time scale. His report came at the end of February 1927 and was quite brief – Perth had to replace its 22 year old trams with new buses; there was no contest. Renewals for track were estimated at £19,126 but the single track and loop arrangement created severe limitations, restricting speed and all the (by now, poor condition) point-work caused wear and tear to the vehicles. A tram's life, he advised, was not more than 20 years; Perth's were 22 years old and while they had been well maintained they were tired and their equipments were out of date and inefficient compared to more modern vehicles. This was exactly what the Convener of the Tramways Committee, Colonel H Dalton Henderson wanted to hear; he was a convinced bus enthusiast so Pilcher's report was embraced eagerly. It has to be said that 'first generation' electric tramways – particularly of the small size typified at Perth were now coming to the end of their lives. Most had been run down during the war period and both track and vehicles were in need of renewal. The Kilmarnock Corporation lines had recently been replaced by buses. In large cities which benefitted from economies of scale tramways survived, generally until a similar scenario followed after the end of the Second World War. After the cessation of the First World War the market was flooded by large numbers of de-commissioned lorries which easily converted into basic passenger carrying vehicles.

At this time a bill was posted in Corporation vehicles: 'When going out and when going home travel in your own tram and 'bus. You own this car.' All too little; too late. The Convener and the Transport Manager attended the Scottish Motor Show in Glasgow's Kelvin Hall on 10th November and arranged for demonstrator buses to be in Perth for Monday 14th. Thornycroft's ability to supply virtually immediately was the deciding factor, and the vehicles ordered were put in service as they arrived, on the Scone to Cherrybank route, allowing withdrawal of two trams on 22nd November 1927. It was intended that a phased and gradual change would take place until such time as the bus operational limitations of the 1908 legislation were updated. However, this had been upset by the appearance on the scene of a voracious competitor and the commencement of the 'Perth Bus War'. The machinations of this organisation, the Perth General Omnibus Company are dealt with below. Suffice to say that the travelling public of the 'Fair City' had never had it so good. In a short space of time they had moved from an ancient tram service, to two competing bus operators – and still had some trams. However, this situation lasted less than a year until the interloper was bought off by the Corporation.

Most trams were now running completely empty and from 11th January 1928 the Scone service was limited to operate morning and evening only, with most trips running Fitzroy Terrace to Rose Crescent only. There was just one daily run to each terminus, for workers at 12.30 pm. On both of the other routes, a single car gave a minimal service at meal times; Sunday trams ended at this time also. Just four cars were required for operations (necessary to comply with the 1908 legislation) with a fifth retained for spare. To make space for buses at Scone, the seven surplus cars were driven to the end of the Craigie line, then onto rails laid loose on the road and into the Council yard at Craigiehaugh. The remaining cars ran occasionally to validate bus operations as within three miles of a tram route, while Royal Assent was waited for the Order allowing the Corporation to operate buses without restriction. During February 1928 the manager, Mr Snell was forced to resign on grounds of ill-health. One cannot help but question if this was exacerbated by the state of unarmed combat which he had been required to endure during the unpleasant period of unbridled competition. His place was taken by Mr W J H Penman, a traffic superintendent with Edinburgh Transport, the appointment being on a temporary basis until September, when it was confirmed.

After August 1928 only two trams were serviceable, making occasional forays along rapidly rusting rails – much to the surprise of other road users – until the final unannounced trip on Saturday 19th January 1929. Ten days later these last two cars were driven to Craigie then pulled off the rails and over the setts into Craigiehaugh yard by a Corporation steam roller; power was then turned off. The saloons of the cars were sold off and appeared in the countryside in various guises. One became a shelter at Craigie terminus (the entire cost met by ex-Bailie J K Taylor) while the Lomond Hotel in Glenfarg took one for a summer house, and car 6 served for decades as a pleasant garden retreat in Balbeggie. A well-meaning attempt to acquire this and restore it to its 1905 glory sadly eventually came to naught.

With what might have appeared to be unseemly haste, a start was made lifting tram rails from Scone Road in July 1929, the entire removal completed in less than a year. Overhead standards were removed from Perth Bridge, but were generally retained for street lighting purposes, many still in use 40 years later. In central streets 'rosettes' fixed to buildings were used to support the overhead and while many of these have been removed over the years, there are still a considerable number for the enquiring eye to find, perhaps the only visible relic of Perth's trams.

Postcard publishers must have been fully occupied in 1906, recording the new phenomenon, the electric tram in its Perth context. Here car 5 is making its westward way over the bridge, through the town and on to Cherrybank. The handsome lines of Smeaton's bridge are well seen, with the cast iron balustrades dating from the widening of 1869. The footways were then cantilevered out from the original structure. Low water in the river shows gravel beds, exploited commercially by dredging further downstream.

Looking back to Bridgend, with a well-laden car proceeding west. The large tree was removed soon after this. Prior to construction of the bridge, the settlement was described as '…a poor paltry village, consisting of a few houses chiefly for the accommodation of boatmen and their families'. This subsequently changed, with the village soon a desirable suburb of Perth, with substantial villas built on ground sloping to the river, and on the rising policies to the south.

Number 12 car, one of the three 'low' cars traverses the bridge during the Edwardian era. For the best part of two and a half centuries this structure has coped with the increasing demands of changing road traffic, always with increasing axle loads. 'Increasing permissible loadings will decrease the number of vehicles' has been the incessant cry from hauliers who paid little or did nothing to mitigate the consequences of road infrastructure damage. The category A-listed pink sandstone bridge carries 21st century traffic assessed at over five million vehicles annually, without weight restriction. Until opening of the Queens Bridge a few hundred yards downstream by Sir Robert Pullar on 13th October 1900 this was the lowest road crossing of the River Tay, but that structure lasted a mere six decades.

George Street, named for King George III, was constructed to give access to the 1771 bridge, and dates from the same period. Many of the late 18th century buildings survive, lending an air of faded refinement. At the far end of the street is the colonnaded frontage of Perth Museum and Art Gallery, built as a home for the Literary and Antiquarian Society. Completed in 1823 its design is intended to replicate the Pantheon in Rome. In George Street the overhead wires for the trams were mostly supported from rosettes fixed to the buildings, some yet in place 90 years after the last tram.

High Street looking west with cars 10 and 11 heading together to the Cross terminus behind the photographer. It was a feature of the early days of electric operation that cars for Dunkeld Road and Craigie left together. As road traffic increased congestion around the Cross also increased, until eventually a decision was made to end this practice, with only one car to be at the terminus at any time. This is probably also a 1906 scene, the section of double line here being lengthened by about 100 yards four years later.

The cross-roads created at the Post Office by Kinnoull Street to the left and Scott Street to the south (on the right) formed a focal point for gatherings on market and feeing days. The length from here to St. John Street was pedestrianised in 1990. The mix of small and large retail outlets in this and surrounding streets has been one of the reasons behind Perth's continuing trading success, but the unassuming regularity of the mostly 18th century buildings was even then being threatened by remarkably out of place 'top-heavy' structures.

Looking east along the High Street towards the Cross terminus, with car 10 proceeding off in that direction. The reason for the gathering seen in this pre-First World War view is unknown, but may be a market day or perhaps a sale at Dan Taylor the hatter's shop? The Council considered that their tramway had four routes; to Scone, to Cherrybank, to Craigie and to Dunkeld Road – all four traversing the High Street. It was hang-over from horse-car days that cars from Scone ran through to Cherrybank.

South Methven Street runs at right angles to the High Street and was used by cars to Cherrybank and to Craigie. The street was laid out in the late 1790s and followed the line of the old west wall of the medieval settlement. Behind the tram in this twenties scene is the imposing building then occupied by Alexander & Brown, Seedsmen, a highly necessary retailer in an agricultural community. Their grand building itself dates from the 1840s and although now converted to flats, surprisingly the distinctive name remains in place. South Methven Street is, like many of Perth's central streets, still home to many small local businesses.

Car 6 is still sufficient of a novelty to attract the gaze in this York Place scene, looking to Kinnoull Hill on the eastern bank of the Tay. On the right the car passes the (then) Perth City & County Infirmary, a purpose built structure opened on 1st October 1838. This building, since 1991 home to the City's much used A K Bell Library and the Archives Department, was vacated by the Infirmary in 1914 then acted as a military hospital until providing a home to County Council Offices for 50 years.

Glasgow Road at the end of Rose Crescent. The original terminus of the horse tramway, where the photograph was taken of the sett layers featured on page 25. The laundry signs seen in that image can be located here also. Rose Crescent was the convenient tram stop for visitors to the new Perth Infirmary which was built behind Rose Crescent on land gifted to the town by the Earl of Kinnoull. The new Infirmary was formally opened by King George V and Queen Mary on 10th July 1914.

Terminus for electric trams at Cherrybank was exactly where had been that for the horse trams. Tram number 9 is seen at the end of the line, a curve which took the vehicle into sight of any intending passenger hurrying down Glasgow Road. Cherrybank was originally a small hamlet on the low road, seen heading off to the left, but the coming of the tramway encouraged development and it became a desirable suburb of the city, the road lined with large villas.

Cherrybank terminus with car 7, in the period before the First World War. The car is literally 'at the end of the line'. It has been fitted with a replacement platform step to a design patented by the manager, Mr Lambert. The steps fitted to the cars on delivery proved unsuitable in use so they were abandoned with six cars fitted with the Lambert design, the remaining six with a design used on the Dundee and Broughty Ferry Company cars.

Dunkeld Road terminus was at the junction of that road with Crieff Road. Car 11 is at the end of the track at the terminus. Although cars operating this route were not constrained by any low bridge, nevertheless it tended – certainly in the first years of electric operation – to be one of the three low cars which was found here. Although the Cross was almost always the city terminus, it was not unknown for cars to run to Bridgend on race meeting days.

Further into town, with car 12 passing the tenements of Readdie's Building on Dunkeld Road. The carved shield recording construction in 1885 is still to be seen on the front elevation. On extreme left, on the corner of Balhousie Avenue, is the ornate lamp outside 4 Myrtle Place indicating the residence of Councilor James M Miller whose music shop was in County Place. In Perth and some other cities, many buildings or groups of buildings were given individual names, but are now numbered as part of the road or street of which they form part.

At South Street Port the tram lines to Cherrybank and Craigie separated; the overhead for the former can be seen on the left of this scene, with car 12 on the run to Craigie. As one of the low cars it is performing a necessary duty, since at the time of the photo, the railway bridge over King Street had not been reconstructed.

The infamous railway over-bridge in King Street, cause of much angst when the electric tramways were being designed, with the alteration in height of the cars being laid at the door of the engineer, who, it was claimed, acted outwith his remit by changing the height of the saloon. The Council maintained that a reduced height made it 'impossible for a man of average height with a tall (top) hat to stand erect'. The bridge was rebuilt, with clearance increased by eighteen inches on 11th March 1907, allowing use of all cars.

King's Place is the westward extension of Marshall Place, together forming the northern boundary of the South Inch. The skyline is dominated by the crown spire of the church of St. Leonard's-in-the-Fields which dates only from 1885, but looks older. It is highly reminiscent of St. Giles Cathedral in Edinburgh.

Having climbed St. Leonard's Bank and crossed the long bridge over no less than eleven railway tracks, the tram route turned into Priory Place. It must be assumed that the 'Priory' comes from the nearby Nunnery of St. Mary Magdalene, which was suppressed prior to the Reformation. This is low car 11, the photo dating from the great photographic catch-up of 1906.

Craigie tram terminus was as shown here, awkwardly situated at the narrow end of Priory Place at Queen Street; the end of the rails can be seen. Normally the tram stood awaiting its timetabled departure on the double track, enabling traffic to pass, it would go to the single track to reverse only. The fact that it was then not visible to approaching passengers was an inconvenience, and a short extension was made in 1910 which also removed, to some degree, the awkward obstruction.

The short extension of less than 100 yards from the Craigie terminus brought the tramways to their maximum length. The new terminus (and most of the extension) is seen here, showing how the track was laid close to the footpath – again to minimise obstruction – not that there seems then to have been much of that. The new terminus was at the end of Windsor Terrace; the gap at the gable end has now been built up.

After the alterations to King Street bridge, but before the extension to Windsor Terrace, 'high' car 6 is posed with driver and conductor at Craigie. Close examination will show the different platform step when compared to car 7 at Cherrybank on page 43.

A covering of snow has altered the aspect of Glasgow Road at Rose Crescent. Tram tracks have been kept clear and what little road traffic there is has kept to the cleared area. If snow was expected one tram, fitted fore and aft with snow-ploughs, would run all night to keep rails clear. Even the horse trams had a basic snow-plough. However, in severe snow storms, if manpower was not sufficient to keep lines open, operation was suspended.

For the Coronation of King George V on 22nd June 1911 several trams in use were decorated and photographed to record the event. Car 5 is posed at the passing loop near Langleybank between Bridgend and Scone giving a good indication of the undeveloped surroundings. This is an aspect which has not changed; Scone is still distinct from Perth, not just physically.

Decorated cars could be arranged (at a cost) for any occasion and various flower shows etc were so advertised. Here is car 1 all lit up in Scone Depot yard on 19th February 1915, drawing attention to a recruiting demonstration to be held that evening in the City Hall.

As men left to fight, shortage required recruitment of women to the tramway crews. Seven conductresses were taken on the books in the summer of 1918. Dundee resisted the change until 1917, but many undertakings found it necessary to call for feminine assistance earlier in the war period. Car 6 is at Cherrybank terminus.

Car 8 with the Scone Depot workshop staff in the 1920s. Although retaining the depot at Scone was probably not a clever idea in relation to the amount of 'dead' mileage consequently required, the village was home to many employees. Figures were produced that nearly 300 miles in each four weeks was unproductive mileage. Cars returning to the depot carried passengers, but had a depot been built in King Edward Street as proposed, savings would have been made. However, recovering the cost of this 'saving' would have taken a considerable period.

Snow scene with tram 4 at Viewlands Terrace, Cherrybank. Only continuous operation of trams kept the lines clear, but it would appear on this occasion shovel-power has been necessary to clear the tracks. This may have been during the heavy snow fall of November 1915; pity the driver on the front platform in such conditions.

A busy scene at South Street Port, looking east from County Place with car 12 turning into South Methven Street. Much more street traffic is now apparent in this 1920s scene, but the heavily patronised tram is still providing a useful service. The tram shows alterations which were not applied to all; the destination indicator box is now below the canopy, making it more convenient for the driver to change without having to climb to the top deck. There is also the panel below the stairs, the purpose of which has not yet been confirmed.

A 1920s view of County Place showing the track deterioration which assisted in giving trams a bad name. Poor maintenance during and after the Great War resulted in a backlog of work to keep rails properly levelled. Joints were a particular problem area and a welding programme was undertaken which proved to be too little, too late.

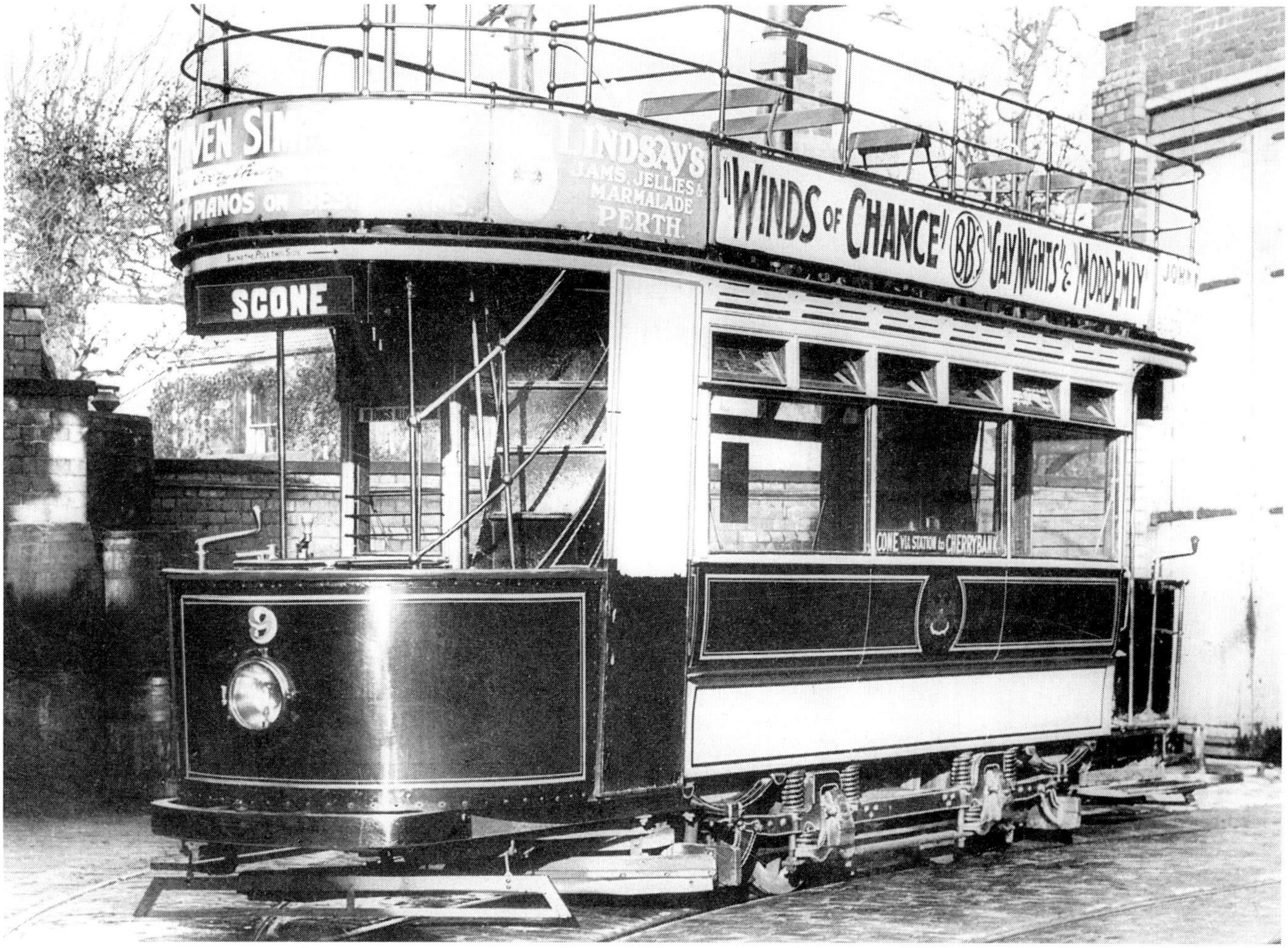

Car 9 in Scone Depot yard shows modifications; the lowered destination box and the panel at the side of the stair. Most (but not all) cars had one or other, or both, applied. The adverts on the upper deck panels give good clues to the date of the photograph. BB's [Bright and Beautiful] was a cinema on Victoria Street from 1913 (now demolished) and *Winds of Chance* was showing there in early 1927. The car is in remarkably good condition for that period – other photos show worn and tired vehicles – but they were then over 20 years old.

The decision for a gradual wind down of the tram system allowed a reduction in the number of working trams. Several cars withdrawn in March 1928 were taken to the Burgh yard at Craigiehaugh. From Craigie terminus, using short lengths of rail and a 'jump lead' they were driven over the road surface into the yard with car 4 here being subjected to this unorthodox practice.

The dreich last day of tram operation, 19th January 1929, with car 6 at Scone Depot, then one of only two operational cars. On the right is conductor Donald Paton, later better known as 'Perth's playwright'. (Photograph courtesy Donald N M Paton.)

Perth Corporation bus services
(1911–1934)

Although power to run buses – in connection with the trams and for only three miles from any terminus – was achieved in 1908 it was three years later before advantage of this was taken. With little or no prior debate a daily service was commenced, probably on 1st May 1911 using a Belhaven charabanc hired from the County Garage in Perth at £10 per week. That this was a good investment was shown immediately by the first week's receipts amounting to £18. Although hired locally, the vehicle (TS437) was owned by the North British Industrial Motor Company of Dundee, but had to be replaced (temporarily?) after just a week following an accident. The service was immediately popular, although considerable annoyance to regular passengers was caused when the vehicle was diverted to deal with private hires and other such work. The problems of having a single vehicle were apparent, but it was some time before another was obtained. On 8th January 1912 press reports note 'the new Almondbank bus … built on handsome and massive lines…', a 30-seat Belhaven (ES632). Later that year, a meal-time only service was started from Dunkeld Road tram terminus to Pullar's Tulloch dye-works a mile out on the Tulloch Road. The run was subsidised by Pullar, male workers paying 9d per week, female workers 6d, possibly a reflection of their respective wage rates. A second-hand Commer charabanc was purchased (for £450) in the summer of 1912, rapidly replaced by a new Commer bus (ES863) that November. This cost £817, but the second-hand vehicle was taken in part-exchange with a discount of £450 allowed. As and when required vehicles were hired from the Industrial Motor Co.

New routes to Balbeggie and Bridge of Earn commenced in early 1913 using the new Commer. The two buses were also used to provide transport to the centuries old Perth Hunt Race meetings, transferred from the North Inch to Scone Palace Grounds in 1908 following the banning of alcohol use at the original site. No further vehicles were added until 1916 when a Lothian bus (ES1970) manufactured by SMT of Edinburgh was obtained on hire purchase. Needed to cope with workers' traffic generated by the war effort, in 1917 it was converted to use town's gas for fuel, contained in a large canvas bag in a timber enclosure on the bus roof. As Scone Depot was now getting overcrowded, garage space was rented temporarily at the Shields Motor Company's premises in Dunkeld Road while plans were drawn up for a central facility in Scott Street for the increasing fleet. At the end of the war, in addition to war workers' special services, regular routes were operated to Almondbank via Tulloch, to Bridge of Earn via Edinburgh Road, and to Balbeggie – this latter initially on only two days per week, with just two journeys per day (later increased to three).

To test demand for a bus service for Almondbank, some 3 miles from Perth, off the Crieff road, in May 1911 this charabanc was hired from the Perth County Garage for £10 per week. They cross-hired it from North British Industrial Motors of Seagate Dundee. It was a Belhaven, built in Wishaw, registered TS437 and is seen on Tay Street.

Having established that it could be a paying proposition the hired charabanc was returned, and a Belhaven bus (ES632) was obtained in January 1912. This image was made very shortly afterwards, in the first week of February 1912 in Main Street, Almondbank outside the post office. The billboard on the wall where the girl is posting a letter refers to the tragic loss of the British submarine A3. Now there is no post office and no wall post-box either.

Valentine operated tours from their King Edward Street premises until that part of the business was acquired by Alexander in 1935. The sales and garage departments of the undertaking lasted until 1983.

Tilling-Stevens ES4474 was purchased in April 1922 and lasted with the Corporation for seven years. The 32 seat body was probably supplied by Strachan & Brown who worked closely with the builders of the chassis and engine. (From collection of Allan T Condie)

Any possibility of extending the tramways was firmly disposed with after the Great War, and four buses were purchased in 1923-24. The last of these was 32-seat Guy, ES6733 of which this appears to be the sole photographic record. Three bus routes were by then operated, to Almondbank, Bridge of Earn, and Balbeggie – the latter less frequently than the other routes.

In the spring of 1920, following numerous requests from locals, a new route was tried to the Jeanfield area. This ran from the Cross (as then did all other town bus services) by way of Old High Street to Goodlyburn for a 2d fare, immediately objected to as excessive. 2d fare for 1¼ miles compared to the same fare for the 1½ miles to Cherrybank was considered totally unfair! The only result appears to have been an increase of fares to Bridge of Earn and Almondbank from 5d to 6d.

At the beginning of 1921 arrangements were made to borrow £20,000 for development of bus operations and the opportunity was taken to assess another two demonstrators. A petrol-electric Tilling-Stevens was being used in Dundee showing that Council how it performed on their steep Constitution Road and it came to Perth on 13th January. The next week a Karrier was seen, but neither of these visits prompted an immediate sale. The next purchase came in April 1922, when a 32-seat Tilling-Stevens bus (ES4474) with a grey livery was purchased for £1,431, bought outright from the Capital Account. It was driven to Perth from the manufacturer's works in Maidstone with Mr Snell accompanying it on what amounted to a 'proving' run; it performed impeccably. Despite this success, the next purchase was a 26-seat Guy (ES5696) got in July 1923 for £1,075.

A Guy demonstrator came for a short time early in 1924 and a deal was done in the middle of that year when the original elderly Belhaven and Commer were theoretically replaced by another 32-seat Tilling-Stevens (ES6732) and another Guy (ES6733) also 32-seat, although the two old buses were retained for a time. These new vehicles were known as Tilling-Stevens No 2 and Guy No 2, both painted maroon and cream. The special service to Pullar's Tulloch Works, was a good earner, but the original (rather discriminatory) fare scheme was replaced by a deal where special tickets were issued to Pullar at 1d each who sold them to their workers at half-price. Pullar was a particularly demanding client, with requirements determined by changing seasonal shift patterns and demands often exceeding availability of vehicles. In 1927 the two Guys, then the two Tilling-Stevens, were fitted with pneumatic tyres. About this time another small garage near the city centre was acquired, in Charles Street.

Perhaps anticipating the situation, two local bus proprietors seized the opportunity to move in. Peter Crerar from Crieff already operated from that town and similarly David Hepburn operated to Blairgowrie; both had vehicles from their summer operations sitting unused. They combined resources to create the Perth General Omnibus Company [PGOCo] which, with no prior warning, commenced operating in direct competition with the trams on the Scone to Cherrybank route on Monday 7th November 1927, with four vehicles. This was the very day of the Council meeting to decide the future of the Corporation trams, which resolved to effect a gradual change-over. However events overtook this plan. The first salvo in the ensuing war was fired on the 8th, when Corporation fares were reduced by a third, to match the PGOCo's which had started at this cut-throat level. Meantime, the Convener of the Tramway Committee with Mr Snell visited the Glasgow Motor Show and arranged for a Thornycroft demonstrator bus to be in Perth as soon as possible, with a potential order for nine vehicles as a strong inducement. This bus arrived just four days later and was promptly purchased then put in service on the 16th between Scone and Cherrybank, with an immediate order placed for six Thornycrofts, three of 30 (actually 32) seats (the demonstrator being one of these) at £1250 each and three smaller with 20 seats at £980, with delivery as quickly as possible. All except one had arrived by the end of the month and were put on the same route, allowing reduction of the tram service. The final 20-seat bus went into service in December on a new route from the Cross to Darnhall Drive introduced on 7th November using one of the older vehicles. The PGOCo then put a bus on the Craigie route, immediately replicated by the Corporation. Faced with a bewildering choice of new vehicles, the spoiled potential passenger (who had never before experienced such choice – and never would again) deserted the trams, to such a degree that after just two weeks of the 'war' tram takings had dropped by over £90 per week.

In February 1928 a brazen offer was made by the owners of the PGOCo to purchase the Corporation's Transport Department for a lump sum of £9,500 plus an annual 'rent' of £500, in return for exclusive rights to operate within the Burgh boundaries. This was dismissed, the Corporation considering that it did not have powers to grant such monopoly. This opinion was apparently considered differently some six years later. By the summer the following bus routes were operated by the Corporation: Scone to Cherrybank (every 10 minutes), Cross to Craigie and to Darnhall Drive (each 20 minute frequency, giving a 10 minute combined service to Craigie Post Office) Cross to Jeanfield (every 15 minutes, with an extension to Burghmuir every hour) Cross to Claremont Place Crieff Road (every 15 minutes). A part-day service ran Cross to Tulloch, with in addition Pullar's specials with six buses running to different termini – run to suit shifts which varied at different seasons of the year; stopping times could vary from 5 to 8 pm. In addition the last two trams ran Fitzroy Terrace to Rose Crescent during rush hours with one run extended to Cherrybank and one to Scone; one tram ran at rush hours on Dunkeld Road and one during the same periods on Craigie. The Almondbank and Bridge of Earn routes were considered as part of the tram system with one bus on each route.

In an endeavor to recover some degree of control, Perth Council proposed, under the Burgh Police Act, to introduce bus bye-laws, the 'opposition' having taken full advantage of the lack of any such provision. All the tricks of unfair competition were deployed by the in-comers against the established order – fares were slashed; buses chased one another, ran just one minute ahead of the Corporation's published timetables but operating with no timetable of their own operations. Reckless racing, cutting in front of, and picking up passengers waiting for Corporation buses was rife, as was turning out passengers short of the terminus to turn to pick up customers on the opposite side of the road if there was a worthwhile load waiting. Passengers benefitted from the PGOCo 1d fares, these being copied immediately by the Corporation. On no occasion did the PGOCo attempt to introduce a new route – all their endeavours went to duplicating existing services. On an annual basis, Corporation earnings dropped from 13.45d per mile to 6.15d. Approval to the new bye-laws was given by the Scottish Office for implementation on 13th August.

Perth Council applied for a Provisional Order to allow the tram system to be closed and for protection from predatory buses, but only along what had been the former tram routes. Included also was further borrowing power for bus purchase, for a new garage, and for road reinstatement. In order that the bus department would not have to carry the accumulated debt incurred by the tramways, the Order allowed for a special fund, the 'Tramway Debt Redemption Fund'. Objections were registered – unsurprisingly – by the proprietors of the PGOCo, plus the railway companies, Motor Trade Associations and two of the 'Bus Combine' long distance operators (the General Motor Carrying Co of Kirkcaldy and the Scottish General Omnibus Co of Larbert). It had been an unwritten convention that long distance bus operators did not lift or set down passengers within the Corporation area. The County Council made objections relating to road lighting and reinstatement of the road between the City boundary and the top of Scone, but agreement with them was reached prior to the hearing. An Inquiry into the Order commenced in Edinburgh on 24th July 1928, chaired by Lord Chalmers. After hearing a lengthy submission on behalf of the Corporation, the case for the opposing parties commenced with an announcement that basic agreement had been achieved. After lunch, Counsel for the objectors, now reduced to just the PGOCo, announced that complete agreement had been achieved during the protracted break. The Bill then progressed unopposed.

Tramway employees became the staff of the Transport Department from January 1929, just as soon as the last tram had run and are recorded for posterity in Scone Depot yard.

The Corporation's recently acquired bus fleet consisted of Thornycrofts of either 32, 26 or 20 seats; and with the PGOCo take-over (effective 5th August) came a motley selection of disparate vehicles. Scone Depot was unable to accommodate the increase, with some buses again kept in the Shields Motor Co.'s garage. It was intended to provide a new facility to be used by vehicles of all departments, and to this end the old Fechney Industrial School site in Riggs Road was bought. There is some doubt regarding the number of vehicles which came from the PGOCo; first reports refer to eleven, the arbiter (Douglas Hayes, General Manager of the Scottish General Omnibus Company of Larbert) valued thirteen but the Council in October specified twelve were to be taken, five Lancia, five Gilford, one Dodge and one Karrier. The Corporation's buses now numbered 32 vehicles, with 11 types of engine and fourteen types of body. Some of the PGOCo vehicles proved unreliable and the Lancias were soon traded-in against more Thornycrofts. At the end of 1928 Perth issued licences for buses operating into the Burgh amounting to no less than 475 vehicles from twelve operators. As an indication of the mushroom expansion of motor bus operation at this period, the corresponding figure two years later was 845 from nineteen operators.

The Corporation, having announced that they were giving up the trams, were met with an opportunist rival operation, the Perth General Omnibus Company, duplicating routes and employing all possible predatory tactics. The new company was formed by David Hepburn and Peter Crerar, both established, but separate operators. This is an earlier 1923 Lancia of Hepburn's outside his bus office at 13 High Street. The historic carved pediment on the left dates from 1699 and can be admired to this day.

Peter Crerar, the other partner, was an established vehicle body-builder and bus operator based then in Leadenflower Street, Crieff. He was agent for many vehicle marques and registered most of his vehicles in Perthshire, including those intended for sale. Six 19-seat charabancs are seen in Lauder Park. On the left are four French Cottins et Desgouttes chassis, on the right two Italian Lancias. Registrations range from ES4742 to ES5010 all dating to 1922, and all appear to have been built for onward sale.

When the Corporation let the contract to Frank Hodgson for bus advertising in December 1928 32 vehicles were referred to, indicating that the twelve ex-PGOCo vehicles were then being utilised. Five Lancias were taken by Thornycroft as part-payment for their 1929 order. The Corporation's bus fleet was recorded thus:

	Dec 1928	April 1929	Dec 1930
Thornycroft 32 seat	4	9	9
Thornycroft 26 seat	6	6	6
Thornycroft 20 seat	6	6	6
Gilford 26 seat	4	4	4
Gilford 30 seat	1	1	1
Karrier 36 seat	1	1	1
Dodge 20 seat	1	1	1
Lancia 20 seat	5	5	0
Tilling-Stevens 32 seat	2	2	1
Guy 32 seat	1	1	1
Guy 30 seat	1	1	0
TOTAL	**32**	**37**	**30**

The unannounced competition took the Corporation totally by surprise, and the Manager rushed off to the Motor Show in Glasgow and arranged for demonstrators to be sent forthwith. The demonstrater Thornycroft arrived first, was successful, and started an association which lasted several years. This official photograph, taken on the South Inch, shows thirteen of their products, probably taken in July 1928. The demonstrator OT6363 is fifth from the far (right) end. From the left are GS38, ES9949, GS37, ES9550, GS36, ES9951, GS368, ES9944, OT6363, ES9943, GS141, GS142, and GS179. (From collection of Geoff Lumb).

Corporation buses displayed a large 'T' above the destination screen, illuminated at night, to identify them as from the Transport fleet. Other operators were expected to follow suit; buses of Armstrong of Spittalfield carried a large letter 'A'.

As soon as the last tram had wrought its unremarked journey, the department was rebranded as 'Transport' with new staff uniforms. Cap badges were issued, probably to the same design as used by the Burgh police. As the city developed, in particular by central slum clearance plus new peripheral housing schemes, the necessary bus services followed; to give assistance a route numbering system was introduced in August 1930; no details of this have been uncovered. Despite trade depression passenger numbers increased and at the end of 1932 it was decided to purchase four 48-seat double-deck buses for the Scone to Cherrybank run. Two were petrol-engined from Thornycroft with metal bodies by Metropolitan-Cammell Weyman (MCW), the other two by Crossley of Manchester with diesel engines and timber-framed bodies from Pickering of Wishaw. The two Crossleys arrived first and were put in service on 22nd July 1933, while the Thornycrofts were not delivered until the end of August. These were not immediately successful, making several return journeys to their suppliers for modification. The Pickering bodies were found to be heavy with some top deck seats temporarily removed, then all seats were replaced by a lighter design. Rationalisation of the fleet continued with a decision to concentrate on petrol-engined Thornycroft single-deckers plus diesel-engined, metal bodied, Crossley double-deckers. Despite this, the next order to be placed – during March 1934 – was for four single-deck Albions with Gardner diesel engines and 32-seat locally built Cadogan bodies. It was intended to purchase two more Crossley double-deckers, but this order was not confirmed.

At the end of March Mr Penman accepted an appointment in Lancaster (perhaps not unrelated to the purchase of Albion against his recommendation) followed almost immediately by receipt of an unsolicited letter from Messrs Walter Alexander and Company dated 14th April, asking if the Corporation would be prepared to dispose of their bus undertaking to them. The very suggestion that a valued municipal asset should be sold to what was seen as private enterprise was sufficient to stir the radicals of the Fair City. After word spread and a Council debate was held on 14th May, a noisy protest meeting was held in the High Street outside the Council Chambers organised by the Independent Labour Party, the Communist Party and the Perth Unemployed Association. After the meeting the protesters sent a resolution to the Council demanding full details be made public, and that ratepayers should be allowed to express their opinion. The National Union of Railwaymen and the Perth Trades and Industrial Council both submitted similar resolutions. The outcome was that from three choices – acceptance immediately, indefinite delay or a two week moratorium – the latter was agreed. It was stated that even with the trams gone, bus operations were a drain on rates to the extent of almost £9,000 per annum, or 8d in the £ on the rates. Alexander's offer was made public and noted that this would dispose of burden of the Tram Debt Redemption Fund, would pay the debt on the cost of Riggs Road Garage. Also, the annual payment would, with these costly debts removed, allow operations to make an estimated contribution to the rates of around 3d in the £. Perth Trades Council rallied trade unionists, forming the Perth Ratepayers Protest Association to organise opposition to any sale, petitioning that the undertaking be retained as a municipal asset. A protest rally was held in the City Hall on Sunday 27th May, prior to the decision-making Council meeting two days later. A resolution was prepared on the grounds that '…the best interests of the citizens could only be served when an undertaking of this nature is owned and controlled by the municipality'.

When an increased offer was accepted by 17 votes to 7 the citizens of Perth were so roused that the Lord Provost required a police escort from the Chambers, but in fact the steam seems to have gone out of the protest after the details were made public. The price was increased to £22,000 plus the unaltered rent of £1,500 p.a. for 21 years. The lease could thereafter be renewed at seven yearly intervals, or revert to the Corporation. All fares would remain as they were, or adjusted only by agreement; services were to be no less than existed, but could be extended or varied also by agreement; also all employees below the age of 60 were guaranteed re-employment. It did not seem a bad deal, and most opposition except from die-hard anti-capitalists was subdued. A major aspect of the agreement gave Alexander exclusive operational rights within the Burgh, plus the Corporation would use their best efforts to ensure that continued in the future. Alexander's cheque was duly received on 14th June, followed by a brief ceremony at Riggs Road five days later. The book-keeping date of transfer was backdated to 15th May 1934. Day to day operation of Perth Corporation's bus department was put in the hands of William Gray, former foreman at Riggs Road. This agreement followed closely that of May 1931 relative to Alexander's takeover of the Kirkcaldy tram system.

Neither agreement stipulated a requirement that vehicles on local services should be painted in a distinguishing livery. It is considered that Alexander chose to maintain a red livery for these vehicles to differentiate them for benefit of local passengers, as there were occasions where the local fare schedule differed from that of long distance operations over the same section of route. In Kirkcaldy, buses on town services were also painted red. Details of Alexander's vehicles which have carried the distinctive Perth livery are given in Allan Condie's publications, to which the reader is directed.

Perth area bus services (some for workers only and some infrequent) operated by the Corporation and transferred to Alexander were: Cherrybank (Oakbank Road) & Scone (Mansfield Road or Highfield Road); City Hall & Hillyland; City Hall & Crieff Road (Claremont Place); City Hall & Balthayock; City Hall & Aberdalgie; City Hall & Stormontfield; King Edward Street & Bridge of Earn; King Edward Street & Rhynd; High Street (The Cross) & Craigie; GPO & Barnhill; GPO & Gas Works; Kinnoull St & Almondbank; Kinnoull St & Pitcairngreen; Kinnoull St & Tibbermore; Darnhall Drive & Hillyland or Tulloch Terrace; Darnhall Drive & Claremont Place; Fitzroy Terrace & High Craigie; Drummond Crescent & Jeanfield or Burghmuir; Rose Crescent & Goodlyburn; South Street Port & Pullar's Works (Tulloch); Kinnoull Street & Muirton Park; King Edward Street & Kinnoull Hill; plus also Excursions and Tours.

Alexander undertook to accept the six vehicles the Corporation had ordered, which could theoretically have been those (Leylands) which appeared the following year carrying Perth registrations GS5001-6. It has also been stated that three of the ordered Albions became WG2384-6 and were used as part of Alexander's Perth 'red' fleet. In Corporation days Riggs Road garage was also used for vehicles of other departments, with electricity vans, gas department vehicles, cleansing lorries etc being maintained there. Two Morris cars used by all departments on a common-user basis were also kept here.

Altercation in Glasgow Road at the red sandstone offices of Arthur Bell, whisky distillers, in May 1928. The small Thornycroft has ended on the footpath, and in the rear, bringing assistance is Demonstrator number 1, with its high panel below the driver's cab.

This scene can be dated fairly accurately to the summer of 1928. The bus was new in March of that year while the tram track and overhead were removed before a further year had passed. Thornycroft GS142 is picking up a covey of lassies, all probably heading for Pullar's cleaning and dyeing works at Tulloch. The location is Atholl Street on the Dunkeld Road route, with St. Ninian's Episcopal Cathedral on the left side, notable as the first cathedral building commenced after the Reformation.

(From collection of Allan T Condie)

High Street at the Post Office, immediately after the tram rails were removed in the summer of 1929. Corporation bus (GS36) is a Thornycroft with a locally-built body by Cadogan, new in January 1928 which was included in the Transport Department assets passed to Alexander in 1934. Daniel Cadogan was a former Crerar employee who set up on his own in 1924 and had vocal support on the Council for all such work to be kept for local employers.

Thornycroft UB registered GS368 came in June 1928 with a 32 seat body built by Ransome Simms and Jeffries of Ipswich, it was numbered 4 in the Corporation fleet. The illuminated letter 'T' above the destination box indicated to passengers that this was one of 'their own' buses to encourage its use.

GS616 of September 1928 was a Thornycroft BC with a 26 seat Cadogan Perth-built body. Numbered 5 in the Transport Department fleet, it passed to Alexander in 1934 with the assets of the department and went on to be renumbered O250, but lasted with them for just one year.

South Street Port (at the west end of South Street) seen enjoying a weak winter sun in December 1931. Bus number 6 (GS641) seen coming in from Craigie is yet another Thornycroft with Cadogan body. This was in service in October 1928 and with the others went to Alexander in 1934, but was soon disposed of.

A one-off in the fleet which passed from Hepburn to the PGOCo to the Corporation was this long Karrier which was given a 36-seat Crerar body. Karrier, of Penistone, Huddersfield, was created in 1920 as an offshoot of Clayton & Company, and in addition to buses and trolley-buses built many specialised municipal vehicles. This bus was registered ES9288 in May 1927 but was withdrawn by the Corporation in 1934 just prior to Alexander's involvement, so was not included in the stock taken by them.

During the short period that the Karrier was used by Perth Corporation it was photographed with its crew at Scone terminus. Corporation fleet number 27 is prominent on the waist panel. It did not fit with the Corporation's vehicle philosophy and was withdrawn at the start of 1934. The Transport Department, re-named early in 1929, then adopted a cap badge of the City's coat of arms.

(From collection of Allan T Condie)

Summary of events post 1934

Regulation of bus services was now in the hands of area Traffic Commissioners appointed under the Road Traffic Act and at their May 1935 meeting they minuted appreciation of the quality and efficiency of the service being provided. 'Messrs Alexander have gone out of their way to try to meet the needs of the public in every direction. They have given far better services to parts of the city that had previously never been catered for'. Such fulsome praise was hard to come by, but possibly reflected the pride which was still exhibited by many former Corporation employees, acknowledging their endeavours to serve the city well. The Commissioners heard applications for new services etc. then published their findings in *Notes and Proceedings* which form a continuous record of intentions – perhaps not always what actually transpired.

Service changes followed as the city expanded and as traffic patterns altered. In the late 1930s the operating company wished to relieve themselves of the local element of the ex-Corporation route to Bridge of Earn, which on occasion had only four passengers. It was stated since daily 60 to 80 long distance buses used the same road, these could easily accommodate the sparse local need. This was not accepted by the Commissioners who required that the service be continued, but kept under review. Despite a 500 signature petition in February 1938 the Craigie route was altered; previously following the old tram track this was altered to operate from King Edward Street, South Street, Scott Street and King's Place, inconveniencing many people.

Alexander pursued an active programme of vehicle refurbishment with extensive purchase of second-hand buses which were reconditioned or rebuilt in their Falkirk workshops or Stirling coachworks. Many such specimens – generally Albions – reached the Perth 'red fleet' in the inter-war years, and vehicles appeared in local deployment which had started their lives as far away as Exeter or Carmarthen. However by the early 1940s even this second life was coming to the end of its tenure and these old rebuilds were in some cases replaced by small brown wooden-seated utility Bedfords of which Riggs Road received six in 1943. After the end of the war these achieved the local red colours, the final single-deck vehicles so distinguished. The use of the red livery for single-deck buses petered out around 1953 with the last of these small Bedfords. Thereafter only local service double-deck vehicles were so identified – but this did not stop them being used for special or extra workings, popping up as far afield as Dundee or even Glasgow. While a number of second-hand and/or rebodied Leyland Titans were drafted in during the early thirties for the Scone run, these were mostly replaced in 1945 by Guy Arabs (many second-hand from London) which provided the mainstay until replaced in their turn in 1959 by Bristol Lodekkas. The first of these came in the local colours, but major changes were afoot which ensured that these were the last to carry the distinctive Perth red livery which after the early '60s soon became a memory. Detail of individual vehicles is given in publications by Allan T Condie.

In 1961 the Alexander's board of directors decided that the company should be split into three operational entities, Midland, Fife and Northern. Perth came within the Midland ambit with the distinctive Perth fleet colours discontinued. The 21 year lease of the city's bus undertaking came to its natural end on 15th May 1955, but allowed for an optional extension at every seven years thereafter. The final payment of £1,500 was made on that date, and the lease was not further extended. The sum was entered in the City Accounts for the 'Privilege of Running Buses' and the relevant clause of the lease stated clearly '…the Company … as long as they continue to supply the transport services under this Agreement, shall make to the Corporation an annual payment…' No identifiable payment appears in the accounts subsequently and no form of explanation for this termination of payment – which appears to have no limit of time – has been located. No proposal to invoke an extension has been traced. It has to be construed that the payment was made 'so long as they continue to supply the transport services under this Agreement' and that since the Agreement had terminated, so had the payment. This is probably not the original intent of the Agreement which allowed for seven-yearly extensions, but by this time the Council had no intention of reverting to become bus operators again. By 1955 virtually all national bus services were operated by the state through assorted operating companies; in Perth and surrounding area the same 'named' operating company still traded, now as Walter Alexander & Sons (Midland) Limited.

A few exceptions remained to this generalisation, however, and at the time Perth benefitted from operation by two well-established public service providers who added variety to the largely standardised operations and fleet of the major supplier; these were Bankfoot Motor Services and A&C McLennan of Spittalfield, to whom we will return.

The last vehicles to appear in Perth Corporation livery were four 48-seat double-deckers for the Scone to Cherrybank route. Two were from Thornycroft with Metropolitan Cammell Weymann bodies, while the other two were by Crossley with bodies by Pickering of Wishaw. This Thornycroft (GS3917) became fleet number 30, then Alexander RO261 after 1934. It was photographed in Park Street South Glasgow.

With its new owners GS3917 lasted a little longer than many of the buses acquired from the Corporation. In the red 'PCT' livery adopted for the town routes, it is seen at the foot of Oakbank Road Cherrybank showing route number '2' for Scone; route numbers were introduced in the summer of 1930. The photo dates from after 1936 when it was renumbered as RO81, then withdrawn in 1938.

At the same locus, on the same day, Leyland Titan WG3382 (R48) of March 1935 vintage is in the red PCT colours, which it retained until transferred elsewhere at the end of 1945. No route number is on display, this initial scheme not surviving for long.

In the same way as Perth became a natural hub for railway operations, it became, in the years following the First World War, a natural focal point for road transport development. With a large number of war surplus lorry chassis on the market, and many trained drivers demobilised, it was a natural progression for these talents and these resources to merge to form the basis of a new, unregulated, industry. While railways joined centres of population, this was often at the expense of smaller villages on the route. Stations, where provided, were not infrequently at considerable distances from the communities nominally served, so here was potential. The old Balbeggie and Scone horse bus had for three decades given a link to Perth markets and the station, and the indication of the future trend was apparent, with Scone and Balbeggie still having no other rail connection. The Corporation pioneered the 1911 service to Almondbank, which has continued – albeit with changes of operator – right to the present date, with an hourly bus (route 14) now also serving Pitcairngreen, operated by Stagecoach, the transport giant with its roots and headquarters in Perth.

Until Perth Council took a measure of interest and attempted to impose some limited degree of control and started issuing their own licences in 1928, their only regulation was to decide bus stances, most often at Tay Street which became a busy interchange point. From here services radiated to all points of the compass, but virtually all of these services worked inwards, by operators based outwith the City. There was no major Perth-based bus or coach operator following the example of, for instance, of the General Motor Carrying Company from Kirkcaldy, or the Scottish General Omnibus Company of Larbert creating a similar network of local and long distance services. In April 1923 William Armstrong started running in from Spittalfield on Saturdays using a converted Ford lorry. By the early 1940s his business had grown and ran also to Dunkeld and Blairgowrie, but as none of his family opted to succeed him, after his retirement in April 1945 the undertaking passed to his engineer, Sandy McLennan. The 'C' of A&C McLennan was, perhaps unusually, Sandy's wife Catherine – known as May. This was another successful enterprise which over the years maintained to a very high standard a fleet consisting generally of second-hand vehicles. The company had its own body-building workshop and paintshop and their distinctive dark blue and white vehicles were normally to be found in pristine condition – in some cases vastly improved on the manner in which they were presented by their original owners. From their stance in Kinnoull Street regular services ran to Spittalfield while their Errol working departed from the east end of Canal Street. McLennan themselves fell to the Stagecoach empire in 1985, one of the earliest of their acquisitions.

A Dundee service had been acquired with the business of Allan & Scott from Stanley in 1946, who also operated from Stanley into Perth. Allan & Scott had operated a service to and from Errol from 1927, while services serving the Carse of Gowrie villages had been pioneered running from Dundee to Perth by Morrison, then with the Northern Transport Company which was in its turn taken over by Allan & Scott in April 1927. Bankfoot Motor Services was the operating title used by A & W Whyte from 1925 for their bus operations from Waterloo into Perth (Kinnoull Street), and also to Perth by Tullybelton. The small undertaking survived, maintaining its independence into the 1960s, using latterly only Bedford vehicles until it was absorbed by Alexander in February 1961.

Perth City commenced licensing individual buses in October 1928, but as this involved each bus of each operator it became an enormous chore, and one difficult to sustain accurately with frequent sales and purchases of vehicles. As an example, in October 1928, twelve operators registered 475 buses and within three years this had increased to nineteen with no less than 845 vehicles – possibly the peak on both counts. For the record, operators working into the city in January 1931 – with the number of buses registered by each were: W Alexander of Falkirk (355); Allan & Scott of Stanley (6); T Allen of Blyth (6); W Armstrong of Spittalfield (3); GMC of Kirkcaldy (88); Kelty Motor Transport (14); J Lamond of Perth (3); Lang of Murthly (2); McKerracher of Aberfeldy (6); Perth Corporation (30); Pitlochry Motor Co (9); SGOCo of Larbert (186); SMT of Dundee (40); Simpson & Forrester of Lochgelly (61); Smith of Kirkcaldy (9); Valentine of Perth (1); Whyte of Bankfoot (4); Westwood & Smith of Edinburgh (5); and A & A Young of Kelty (17).

Other operators who had vehicles registered at other dates included: Clan Motorways of Glasgow; Cormie of Kirkcaldy; Eadie of Markinch; Elliott & Begg of Perth; Finlayson of Broxburn; Fuller of Newburgh; Graham of Stonehaven; Highland Motorways of Glasgow; Holden; W D Laing; Northern General of Arbroath; Penman of Bannockburn; and Peter of Milnathort. The position resolved rapidly after this time of chaos and other than the two local 'independent' operators mentioned above, all services, long or short distance operating into and out of Perth were brought under control of W Alexander & Sons. Competitors were either bought up or metaphorically run off the road (sometimes not just metaphorically).

The Stagecoach Group has used Perth as a base since founded in 1980. The first service, rapidly grasping the principles of Maggie Thatcher's deregulatory philosophy as put into law by the 1980 Transport Act, was from Dundee, via Perth, to London. From this has rapidly emerged a global empire which at one time extended to running the vintage tram service in Portugal from Sintra to Praia das Maçäs north of Lisbon (which has since passed into the hands of the local authority).

In a bizarre twist, Perth acquired a tramcar again in July 2010 when a Blackpool 'Balloon' style double-decker tram was purchased and brought north by Ptarmigan Transport Solutions [PTS] of North Muirton Estate. It was intended to convert it to become a lecture room but events prevented this. Number 235 was built in 1935 and ran in the Lancashire seaside resort until withdrawn in 2003 with major defects. PTS was founded in November 2004 by Stuart Newing-Davis who acquired the Bankfoot Motor Service – at one period branding it as 'Stag-coach'! Some vehicles even carried a livery similar to that of the other company, with legal action promptly following. A bona fide David and Goliath situation, but nobody could emulate or take on the leaders in that field. He soon blotted his copy-book by claiming excess concessionary fare subsidies relating to Bankfoot Buses, but then diversified into the supposedly lucrative sphere of personnel training and labour hire. The 'Train People' and 'Rail Force Recruiting' subsidiaries of the PTS were, he claimed, propping up the parent group, but unfortunately HMRC did not accept this, referring to "years of obfuscation" when he was accused (and convicted) of VAT fraud to a considerable degree.

His plan to adapt the old Blackpool tram as a lecture room was not top priority and when the liquidator was eventually pulled in at the end of 2013, it was soon advertised on eBay – for no less than £8,000. Perhaps unsurprisingly – although interest had been expressed in potential restoration of the seventy-plus year old vehicle – it failed to sell, with the tram last heard of mouldering in a Kirkcaldy scrapyard – a sad end to Perth's final tram. Considering that quite a number of this style of tram still exist, some operating along the 'Golden Mile' to this day, the restoration scheme may have been little more than a pipedream. Indeed this particular vehicle had been stripped to provide parts to keep others of its design working before it left Blackpool.

Remains of Perth's tram system are not hard to find in the city centre – rosettes for overhead support are to be found in numbers in South Methven Street, High Street and George Street – and there is also one near the foot of St. Leonard's Bank. At Scone nothing remains of the depot, although it was used by the Corporation, then the Territorial Army, for decades after the end of the trams, the rails then still in place. A brick pillar, on the south side of the entrance, is the only surviving remnant from 1905.

It must have seemed, in the first years of the 20th century that having an electric tramway was just what the city of Perth required, just as it must have appeared that the way forward was to replace the old horse bus by a horse tramway ten years previously. But events of ensuing years were to change life and travel in ways which could not be anticipated. In common with other conurbations Perth saw physical expansion in the years following the First World War with a spread of population into new housing in lower density suburbs which all required public transport facilities. The existing tram system by this time was in need of renewal, and while operations had generally produced minor profits, the debt legacy incurred from purchase of the horse tramways, amounting to over £2,000 every year, swung the balance into debt, with relief assistance required from the rates. If comparison is made with Kilmarnock, where a similar sized tram undertaking operated, it is notable that the cost of setting up the electric tramways were over 40% greater in Perth. The financing of this was an unsupportable burden. Perth's small tramway when compared to Kilmarnock's (5 track miles compared to 4¼; 12 cars compared to 14) showed that – in physical terms – it was well and economically run. Income per car mile averaged about 20% greater in Perth, but working expenses per car mile, while initially higher in Kilmarnock, reversed after 1923 to be greater in Perth. Circumstances changed in both operations with bus competition and maintenance costs increasing. Both worn-out systems needed substantial track reconstruction and renewal was investigated but, probably wisely, the decision was made, first in Kilmarnock, then in Perth, to replace the trams by buses. The infrastructure had not been renewed on a planned regular basis – any such intent had been pushed aside by the strictures of the First World War. It was only with the lump sum from Alexander in 1934 that the tramway debt was finally eradicated.

When the Transport Department passed to Alexander several Albion chassis were on order, some being taken and fitted with bodies of their own make. This is one of the three, WG2584 (A5) in King Edward Street, one of several city centre termini. King Edward Street was a relatively recent creation, dating from 1901-02. It had been intended to build a central tram depot here and authority was obtained for a line down the street, which was to be the terminus for Dunkeld Road and Craigie cars.

Left: In April 1923 Bill Armstrong from Spittalfield commenced operations running to Kinnoull Street using this very basic conversion of a Ford truck (SA5599). The successful venture was followed by routes to Blairgowrie and to Dunkeld.

Below: Two of Armstrong's vehicles loading in Tay Street c1931. In front, making for Spittalfield is Leyland Badger GS 2157, followed by GS2094, a Thornycroft on the route to Dunkeld. The Badger was an unusual use for what was essentially a goods chassis. Bodies on these Armstrong's vehicles were by Cadogan of Perth. (From collection of R L Grieves)

By 1935 a fleet of five buses had accumulated, the most recent then being Dodge (GS5324) in the 'garage' on the left. Also on display are Leyland GS3240 and Thornycroft GS2094. The livery was deep blue, while the illuminated 'A' above the destination was to identify your bus after dark. (From collection of R L Grieves)

Messrs Elliott and Begg, originally from Paisley, from the end of September 1926 started a service along the main road from Perth to Dundee (Courthouse Square) via Inchture with a single Reo bus. It was successful, as the other operator (Morrison), took the 'low road' by Errol. A second vehicle came at the end of October, but the fledgling company fell to Alexander on 15th December 1927. (From collection of R L Grieves)

Tay Street became the 'de facto' stance for long distance bus traffic in the late twenties and early thirties and in that period all manner of vehicles of all hues were to be seen jostling for position. Fortunately the volume of other road traffic was then considerably less and road safety awareness was not quite so critical. This 1931 scene shows (with others) a bus belonging to A & A Young of Kelty in Fife who operated to Cowdenbeath from May 1929.

Stanley Fuller of Newburgh operated from that north Fife town from 1922, eventually extending to link Perth with St. Andrews via Cupar. His business was purchased by the General Motor Carrying Coy. of Kirkcaldy in July 1928 including this smart little Commer, FG3660. It ran as seen for five months only, conveniently dating this view to 1928.

Simpson's and Forrester's was formed on 1st October 1929 to amalgamate the businesses of Simpson's Motor Service of Dunfermline (with 27 buses) and A & R Forrester of Lochgelly (29 buses). It became thereafter the Lochgelly based operating 'name' for Alexander. The run to Kirkcaldy was operated jointly with GMC of Kirkcaldy. This started as competition, but after both operators were absorbed by Alexander and the timetables rationalised, this disappeared. The bus is a Leyland, of which both operators had substantial numbers.

Kirkcaldy's General Motor Carrying Company (GMC) was early in the business, commencing a service to Burntisland before the First World War. Their Perth service was originally a joint venture with Fuller of Newburgh, but he was bought out soon afterwards. FG4885 was a large handsome soft-top Commer, new in April 1929, numbered 66 in the company roster.

Also operating from Kirkcaldy to Perth was Smith's Motorways – their route being via Auchtermuchty. Leyland FG 4535 was obtained by Smith in November 1928, having been exhibited at that year's Motor Show in Glasgow. Alexander's acquired the business on 1st June 1931.

Scottish General Omnibus Company of Larbert ran long distance routes which passed through Perth. This example is running from Crieff to Carnoustie via Perth and Dundee. The General took over the routes of Peter Crerar of Crieff (including his steamer on Loch Earn) in March 1928, of which this operation was a logical extension.

Another of the many operators into Perth at this time was A & A Young of Kelty. This bus, Leyland FG6975, was the last vehicle purchased by the independent company. It was new in May 1931, the company being absorbed by Alexander that September. Their route from Cowdenbeath to Perth commenced in May 1929, but was soon extended to Dunfermline at the southern end.

A wet day on Tay Street sees the local scene enhanced by two buses belonging to F & J Mitchell of Luthermuir in Kincardineshire, probably on tour, since a stage service to Perth was not amongst their regular operations. Leyland AG8267 had a very convoluted history, originating in 1932 with Midland Bus services of Airdrie, being acquired by Mitchell in April 1947. Bedford SU4894 was new with Mitchell in November 1947, but was sold on in 1952. Mitchell's operations passed to Alexander in October 1967.

South Street became as important part of the Perth road network following opening of the Victoria Bridge which formed a necessary alternative to the Old Bridge. It was the route for all bus traffic heading west from Tay Street to Auchterarder, Stirling and Glasgow. The famous Salutation Hotel faces up St. John Street, and is said to be the oldest hotel in Scotland. What is not disputed is that it has hosted historical figures, from Bonnie Prince Charlie in 1745 to David Bowie in 1969.

Glasgow Road, the main route leading out of the city to the south, shows clearly the disused former tramway standards. These were retained for street lighting purposes and most lasted for a further 30 years after the date of the photograph. Each had a decorative cast iron base which featured the coat of arms of the city. The villas lining the road were mostly built following extension of the horse tramway out to Cherrybank.

By the late 1930s almost all independent bus companies operating into Perth had been swallowed by Alexander. Exceptions were the Spittalfield-based operations of Armstrong and the Bankfoot Motor Service, the trading name of brothers Alex and Bill Whyte. They acquired their business in 1925 from J C Nicoll, and maintained their independence until succumbing to Alexander in February 1961. Originally operating just to Bankfoot, the run was soon extended to Waterloo, then to Dunkeld – this latter contested by Armstrong and the Pitlochry Motor Company. Outside the Atholl Inn at the north end of Bankfoot, Leeds registered Reo WW7270 waits its starting time.

Whyte's stance for Bankfoot or Waterloo was on Kinnoull Street by Foundry Lane where Bedford CES447 is waiting. The five elderly Bedfords in use at the time of Alexander's take-over were not used by them. The top end of Kinnoull Street was the home of Pullar's Dyeworks who as a consequence of the flammable nature of substances employed, maintained their own fire brigade, whose appliance was housed at the corner of Foundry Lane. (Photo by J. Sinclair)

Remarkably well-kempt for its age, twelve-year old 1949 Bedford CGS766 turning from Kinnoull Street into Atholl Street at the start of its 15 mile journey. After the Second World War only Bedford buses were used by Bankfoot Motor Service, but before the war, some distinctly unusual marques were owned, including AJS and BAT. (Photo by J. Sinclair)

Kinnoull Street was also the starting point for McLennan's route to Spittalfield. Many second-hand vehicles passed through the company, but they always were presented in sparkling condition. This is ex Birmingham Corporation Leyland EOG277 (fleet number 52) in the summer of 1957, also making the turn into Atholl Street with the North Inch to the right. (Photo by J. Sinclair)

McLennan also had their basic Bedfords with AES516 (fleet number 28) loading in Tay Street for its journey via St Madoes to Errol. A separate Errol to Dundee service was operated, with vehicles kept in a small garage in the village. This operation had been commenced by the Northern Transport Company in February 1926 which was then passed to Messsrs Allan & Scott (who also ran Stanley to Perth) in July 1927 and was finally acquired by McLennan in 1946. (Photo by J. Sinclair)

The Perth red local bus service also had wooden seated utility Bedford vehicles; this is WG9864 (W115) which was ran on the town's routes for nine years from January 1943. It is seen with crew at the Tulloch Institute, otherwise the 'Hillyland' terminus. (From collection of Allan T Condie)

On the left, Bedford WG9857 (W108) sits gleaming in this Riggs Road garage view. One Leyland (at least) has the Perth red livery and the local title on the cream waist band. None of the other vehicles can be positively identified. The gantry in use to gain access to the lighting by the entrance doors would incur the wrath of the Safety Department. (From collection of Allan T Condie)

View of Tay Street with the Victoria Bridge behind on a summer Sunday in 1949. On the left an SMT Leyland for Blairgowrie; on the right Bedford WG9863 (W114) then double-deck Guys AMS7(RO544) and AMS275 (RO529). All three are contracted to return workers to the Morenish camp near Killin for workers on the Lawers Hydro-Electric Scheme following a week-end of 'r & r'. The last of these vehicles departed the local scene in 1963. (From collection of Allan T Condie)

On the Cherrybank to Scone run in 1950 is Guy AMS272 (RO526) which was a regular on the local routes from 1944 to 1963 – good service from a wartime build. This High Street scene appears to have been recorded on a Sunday morning, with the blinds drawn on the Boots the chemist branch opposite the post office with Kinnoull Street behind. (From collection of Allan T Condie)

Perth Road, Scone in 1950; the almost total lack of road traffic makes a contrast with today's conditions; the A94 major road to Coupar Angus still bisects the village as it did then. Timber poles carrying telephone wires have disappeared and the old 1905 standards for the tram overhead were eventually replaced. Just to the photographer's right stood for many years the disused former electric tram depot, complete with its fan of rusting rails, but even this has now gone. The approaching bus is Guy AMS272 (RO526).

From 1952/53, Perth was served by a considerable number of these (at least) eight year old Guys formerly with London Transport; most survived for a further ten years use in Scotland. GYL431 (RO711) is closely followed by Bristol Lodekka KWG627 (RD77) new in March 1959 which will ultimately displace the old Guys. The vehicles are loading in Scott Street, following a one-way loop on South Street and South Methven Street to get back to the Old High Street. (From collection of Allan T Condie)

Alexander's bus office in the city was in Murray Street off Kinnoull Street, but it is unlikely that these folk are for the Auchterarder bus. More probable is that this is the queue for the matinee at the adjacent Playhouse cinema. Alexander's Leyland Tiger WG5923 (P405) is prepared for its next run to Auchterarder. Fifty of these, new in 1937, the Coronation year of King George VI, were given a red white and blue colour scheme, becoming known – of course – as the 'Coronations'.

Two former Londoners meet in the perhaps unlikely environs of South Street. A&C McLennan's JXN370 (number 85) is former London Transport Leyland RTL47 of 1949 acquired in 1958, while the Guy alongside is Alexander's GYE95 (RO699) of 1945 arriving in Perth in March 1953. By this time South Street was one-way for traffic (east to west). As a consequence the Scone to Cherrybank route served this street for the first time. Reliance Motors, long a feature here has gone, replaced by an anodyne structure giving pend access to Canal Street. (Photo by J. Sinclair)

A & C McLennan used second-hand buses from a multitude of origins. Here at the Kinnoull Street loading point is former Edinburgh ASC700B. It has lost its chromed 'Edinburgh Castle' badge from the centre of the bonnet, and its appearance was altered by the change from its original madder livery to its new owners' smart deep blue. (Photo by J. Sinclair)

In this line-up at Spittalfield are, from the left, LCK924, unknown, LUC72 and JXN370. For the bus enthusiast it was always a delight to visit Spittalfield, where normally a warm welcome was extended. (Photo by J. Sinclair)

Perth Corporation Buses

New	Reg No.	Make	Body	Seats	Disposal
5/11	(TS437)	Belhaven	?	Ch?	Off hire
1/12	ES632	Belhaven	?	Ch?	11/25 sold
7/12	?	Commer (s/h)	?	?	10/12 trade in
10/12	ES863	Commer	?	B30R	11/25 sold
4/16	ES1970	Lothian	SMT	B31R	4/28 scr
4/22	ES4474	Tilling-Stevens No 1	?	B32R	1/29 scr
7/23	ES5696	Guy No 1	?	B30	1/29
7/24	ES6732	Tilling-Stevens No 2	?	B32–26	12/33
7/24	ES6733	Guy No 2	?	B32	12/33
aq11/27	OT6363	Thornycroft	Ransome	B32D (1)	to WA 5/34 (O246)
11/27	ES9943	Thornycroft	Ransome	B32D (2)	to WA 5/34 (O247)
11/27	ES9944	Thornycroft	Ransome	B32D (3)	to WA 5/34 (O248)
11/27	ES9949	Thornycroft	Cadogan	B20F (19)	to WA 5/34 (T33)
11/27	ES9950	Thornycroft	Cadogan	B20F (18)	to WA 5/34 (T32)
12/27	ES9951	Thornycroft	Cadogan	B20F (17)	to WA 5/34 (T31)
1/28	GS36	Thornycroft	Cadogan	B20F (16)	to WA 5/34 (T30)
2/28	GS37	Thornycroft	Cadogan	B20F (20)	to WA 5/34 (T34)
2/28	GS38	Thornycroft	Cadogan	B20F (21)	to WA 5/34 (T35)
3/28	GS141	Thornycroft	Croall	B26R (10)	to WA 5/34 (O255)
3/28	GS142	Thornycroft	Croall	B26R (11)	to WA 5/34 (O256)
3/28	GS179	Thornycroft	Croall	B26R (12)	to WA 5/34 (O257)
6/28	GS368	Thornycroft	Ransome	B32D (4)	to WA 5/34 (O258)
aq8/28	ES9995	Gilford	Crerar	B26 (22)	Lic. surrendered 1/34
aq8/28	ES9938	Gilford	Crerar	B26 (23)	to WA 5/34 (Y69)
aq8/28	ES9994	Gilford	Crerar	B26 (24)	to WA 5/34 (Y70)
aq8/28	ES9930	Gilford	Crerar	B26 (25)	to WA 5/34 (Y71)
aq8/28	GS94	Gilford	Crerar	B30 (26)	to WA 5/34 (Y72)
aq8/28	ES9288	Karrier	Crerar	B36F (27)	to WA 5/34 not used
aq8/28	ES9929	Dodge	Crerar	B20F (28?)	to WA 5/34 not used
aq8/28	ES6831	Lancia	Crerar	B20F	to Thornycroft 4/29
aq8/28	GD1454	Lancia	Str & Brn?	B26F?	to Thornycroft 4/29
aq8/28	GD2483	Lancia	Str & Brn?	B26F?	to Thornycroft 5/29
aq8/28	GD3763	Lancia	Str & Brn?	B26F?	to Thornycroft 5/29
aq8/28	VA3209	Lancia	?	B26F? (29?)	to Thornycroft 8/29
9/28	GS616	Thornycroft	Cadogan	B26R (5)	to WA 5/34 (O250)
10/28	GS641	Thornycroft	Cadogan	B26R (6)	to WA 5/34 (O251)
10/28	GS642	Thornycroft	Cadogan	B26R (7)	to WA 5/34 (O252)
3/29	GS960	Thornycroft	Cadogan	B32D (8)	to WA 5/34 (O253)
3/29	GS1017	Thornycroft	Cadogon	B32D (9)	to WA 5/34 (O254)
5/29	GS1156	Thornycroft	Cadogan	B32D (13)	to WA 5/34 (O258)
5/29	GS1157	Thornycroft	Cadogan	B32D (14)	to WA 5/34 (O259)
8/29	GS1374	Thornycroft	Cadogan	B32D (15)	to WA 5/34 (O260)
8/33	GS3917	Thornycroft	MCCW	H24/24R (30)	to WA 5/34 (RO261)
8/33	GS3918	Thornycroft	MCCW	H24/24R (31)	to WA 5/34 (RO262)
7/33	GS3939	Crossley	Pickering	H24/24R (32)	to WA 5/34 (RO263)
7/33	GS3940	Crossley	Pickering	H24/24R (33)	to WA 5/34 (RO264)